YOUR
RIGHT
TO REST

POTENTIALS
GUIDES FOR PRODUCTIVE LIVING

Wayne E. Oates, General Editor

YOUR RIGHT TO REST

by

WAYNE E. OATES

THE WESTMINSTER PRESS
Philadelphia

Scripture quotations from the Revised Standard Version of the Bible are copyrighted 1946, 1952, © 1971, 1973 by the Division of Christian Education of the National Council of the Churches of Christ in the U.S.A., and are used by permission.

Book Design by Alice Derr

First edition

Published by The Westminster Press®
Philadelphia, Pennsylvania

PRINTED IN THE UNITED STATES OF AMERICA
9 8 7 6 5 4 3 2 1

Library of Congress Cataloging in Publication Data

Oates, Wayne Edward, 1917–
    Your right to rest.

    (Potentials)
    Bibliography: p.
    1. Spiritual life—Baptist authors. 2. Rest—
Religious aspects—Christianity. I. Title. II. Series.
BV4501.2.O23 1984   248.4′86132   83-26045
ISBN 0-664-24517-X (pbk.)

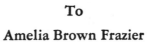

To
Amelia Brown Frazier

Contents

Foreword

The eleven books in this series, Potentials: Guides for Productive Living, speak to your condition and mine in the life we have to live today. The books are designed to ferret out the potentials you have with which to rise above rampant social and psychological problems faced by large numbers of individuals and groups. The purpose of rising above the problems is portrayed as far more than merely your own survival, merely coping, and merely "succeeding" while others fail. These books with one voice encourage you to save your own life by living with commitment to Jesus Christ, and to be a creative servant of the common good as well as your own good.

In this sense, the books are handbooks of ministry with a new emphasis: coupling your own well-being with the well-being of your neighbor. You use the tools of comfort wherewith God comforts you to be a source of strength to those around you. A conscious effort has been made by each author to keep these two dimensions of the second great commandment of our Lord Jesus Christ in harmony with each other.

The two great commandments are given in Luke 10:25–28: "And behold, a lawyer stood up to put him to the test, saying,

'Teacher, what shall I do to inherit eternal life?' He said to him, 'What is written in the law? How do you read?' And he answered, 'You shall love the Lord your God with all your heart, and with all your soul, and with all your strength, and with all your mind; and your neighbor as yourself.' And he said to him, 'You have answered right; do this, and you will live.' "

Underneath the two dimensions of neighbor and self there is also a persistent theme: The only way you can receive such harmony of thought and action is by the intentional re-centering of your life on the sovereignty of God and the rapid rejection of all idols that would enslave you. The theme, then, of this series of books is that these words of Jesus are the master guides both to the realization of your own potentials and to productive living in the nitty-gritty of your day's work.

The books in this series are unique, and each claims your attention separately in several ways.

First, these books address great social issues of our day, but they do so in terms of your own personal involvement in and responses to the problems. For example, the general problem of the public school system, the waste in American consumerism, the health hazards in a lack of rest and vocational burnout, the crippling effects of a defective mental outlook, and the incursion of Eastern mystical traditions into Western Christian activism are all larger-than-life issues. Yet each author translates the problem into the terms of day-to-day living and gives concrete guidelines as to what you can do about the problem.

Second, these books address the undercurrent of helplessness that overwhelming epidemic problems produce in you. The authors visualize you throwing up your hands and saying: "There is nothing *anyone* can do about it." Then they show you that this is not so, and that there are things *you* can do about it.

Third, the authors have all disciplined themselves to stay off their own soapboxes and to limit oratory about how awful the world is. They refuse to stop at gloomy diagnoses of incurable conditions. They go on to deal with your potentials for changing yourself and your world in very specific ways. They do not let you, the reader, off the hook with vague, global utterances and generalized sermons. They energize you with a sense of hope that is generated by basic information, clear decision-making, and new directions taken by you yourself.

Fourth, these books get their basic interpretations and recommendations from a careful plumbing of the depths of the power of faith in God through Jesus Christ. They are not books that leave you with the illusion that you can lift yourself and your world by pulling hard at your own boot-straps. They energize and inspire you through the hope and strength that God in Christ is making available to you through the wisdom of the Bible and the presence of the living Christ in your life. Not even this, though, is presented in a namby-pamby or trite way. You will be surprised with joy at the freshness of the applications of biblical truths which you have looked at so often that you no longer notice their meaning. You will do many "double takes" with reference to your Bible as you read these books. You will find that the Bread of Life is not too holy or too good for human nature's daily food.

The world energy crisis hinges upon our use, misuse, and abuse of nonrenewable energy sources such as fossil fuels. The concern I express in this book is about the most personal, *renewable* resource of energy you and I have, our own physical strength, stamina, and health. Central to our personal energy

crisis is our exercise of our right to rest. Rest, in the harum-
scarum existence of your daily life and mine, is often a low-
rated function. Yet in God's creation of us and in the biblical
script for the drama of a well-lived and well-ordered life, rest
is something indispensable, a necessity.

This book develops the themes of living in harmony with
the pre-established *rhythms* of the days of our years, the
importance of *breathing* for the nourishment and enhance-
ment of our health and energy, the role of fatigue in the
complications of our personal and social lives, and the
importance of sleep in the control of anxiety, indecisiveness,
and pain, and for an accurate perception of the natural and
spiritual world.

The later chapters of the book probe the relation of our
spiritual values and behaviors to the ways in which we either
rest, cannot rest, or will not rest. Restlessness and greed are
corroding partners, and restfulness and freedom from greed
are their opposites. Placelessness and homeless wandering,
without community or calling, take away a sense of serene
restfulness of spirit. Finding your place and purpose in life
restores and sustains your spirit. The life of the spirit at its
best in communion with God is portrayed by the Bible and
known to Christian experience as the "prayer of rest." In this
atmosphere of prayer, rest is the gift of God in Christ.

                                                        WAYNE E. OATES

Louisville, Kentucky

Acknowledgments

I am indebted to the Department of Psychiatry and Behavioral Sciences of the School of Medicine of the University of Louisville for the privilege of six weeks' leave during which I have written this book. I am especially appreciative of the encouragement and permission of Chairman and Professor John Schwab, M.D., in this project.

This book—as is reflected in Chapter 7, on the home as a place of rest—has been written while I have been at home. I am indebted to my wife, Pauline, for her comradeship in the thinking and writing that has gone into these pages. She brings both rest and inspiration to me as she always has in our forty-one years of marriage.

Then, too, the actual logistics of the research and manuscript preparation, and the management of my office, were done by my steadfast friend, colleague, and research assistant, Jenni Khaliel. I acknowledge my deep appreciation for her as a person and as a professional woman. She has made this effort possible in practical terms, and without her work it could not have been done. To her I express my deep gratitude.

W.E.O.

Chapter 1

Your Personal
Energy Crises

The global economic and propaganda struggle over the oil market has monopolized the term "energy crisis." In the home and at the special personal levels of your life and my life we have our own personal energy crises to resolve. That is what this book on your right to rest is all about. You and your friends talk (do you not?) of being exhausted, overscheduled, and fatigued. You see your friends, and maybe find yourself also, eating high-calorie foods, drinking caffeine-loaded beverages, or not being able to sleep as expressions of your inability to rest. At work, we may find that fatigue and exhaustion are the *assumed* way of life of you and your co-workers. Working as I do in a large medical center, I often think that the medical profession itself has made fatigue a permanent way of life. I see much creativity of thought dissipated by fatigue and depleted energy, not only among physicians, but also in business, industry, and education. Yes, the personal energy crisis is at large among us and that is the reason I write, to apprise you of your right to rest.

An Agenda for Facing Your Energy Crises

Let me suggest an agenda for your and my use in self-examination. Understand my covenant with you as my reader: I will suggest problems for our agenda, yes; but throughout the book I will also point to specific ways whereby you can begin now to resolve these problems. Thus you will meet your own personal energy crisis head-on and start replenishing and renewing your energies through the restorative powers of rest.

In our exploration of ways to solve our personal energy crises, my plan is to discuss the following issues as you have to face them each day of your life:

1. Work, wisely done in moderation, makes rest more renewing. Fatigue reduces effectiveness in work.

2. The natural rhythm of your life maintains your alertness and well-being. The rituals of your life bring ease and direction when they are personally chosen.

3. Being out of breath makes rest difficult; your breathing patterns, carefully disciplined, renew your energies.

4. Sleep gathers up the raveling sleeve of care and restores the perspective of your life. It is one of the natural healers of depression. Sleep assuages pain, although much pain over long periods of time causes disorders in your sleep. Settling or "making up your mind" about important decisions enables you to sleep better. Medications are often a short-term gift of God in regulating your sleep, if they are taken with thanksgiving and prayer (I Tim. 4:4–5). Yet medications may become a substitute for actively disciplining yourself to rest naturally. You decide which.

5. Greed, a rarely confessed sin, fuels the fantasy of being

totally at ease. Thus, you and I may mistake ease for genuine rest. We may be carried away with our greed to such an extent that we see no need for sleep.

6. Having a home, a haven, a place to stand with purpose and to be in fellowship with people who accept you and love you is a wellspring of rest.

7. To pray without ceasing is, at its center, to come to rest in God, a rest in God in the midst of the most intense struggles. This is the prayer of rest.

8. Rest is the gift of God in Christ. We are not most alive if always at complete rest. The human heart has its resting and working states that need each other. Not even God's work is ever finally completed. Particular tasks are finished, though. Then God gives the rest that provides the parentheses between tasks well done. The power of the resurrection is the source and pattern for the renewal of life, even after death.

My plan is to discuss each of the above assertions so that they become conversations with you as my reader instead of assertions of my own. I hope to meet you where you are in your day's demands at "the burning of the noontide heat and the burden of the day." I come to you as one who struggles for rest and renewal just as you do.

Fatigue and depletion of energy are no respecters of persons, nor are they limited to one age group or one class of persons.

God is no respecter of persons, either. God enters your and my personal energy crises just as he did in the days of Jesus' earthly ministry. Notice some specific instances of this.

Jesus' Personal Energy Crises

After Herod had John the Baptist beheaded, the work of ministry of Jesus' disciples in their teaching and healing was

all the more strenuous. Jesus "said to them, 'Come away by
yourselves to a lonely place, and rest a while.' For many were
coming and going, and they had no leisure even to eat" (Mark
6:31).

At another time, Jesus "had to pass through Samaria. So he
came to a city of Samaria, called Sychar, near the field that
Jacob gave to his son Joseph. Jacob's well was there, and so
Jesus, wearied as he was with his journey, sat down beside the
well" (John 4:4–6).

You and I often feel distant from God in our fatigue, but
God came near to us in Jesus and experienced our need for
rest and our bone-tired weariness in the days of his earthly
life. You are not alone in your energy crisis.

A Plan of Action

Let me, as an undershepherd of Jesus Christ, open conver-
sation with you, then, in the following pages of this book. Let
us converse about the specific meanings of rest in your life
and some special ways you can go about creating breathing
room, resting space, renewal time to replenish your energies
for the living of these days. I want to move from the concrete
situations that deplete your energies to specific ways to
conserve your resting times and places, to ways in which,
through the disciplines of the spiritual life, you may generate
new sources of strength.

Your human organism, once thought to have a fixed,
genetically coded amount of energy, is now being seen, not as
nonrenewable like fossil energy, but as a *renewable* form of
energy. The prophet Isaiah put it this way:

> Why do you say, O Jacob,
>   and speak, O Israel,
> "My way is hid from the LORD,

and my right is disregarded by my God"?
Have you not known? Have you not heard?
The LORD is the everlasting God,
   the Creator of the ends of the earth.
He does not faint or grow weary,
   his understanding is unsearchable.
He gives power to the faint,
   and to him who has no might he increases
      strength.
Even youths shall faint and be weary,
   and young men shall fall exhausted;
but they who wait for the LORD shall renew their
      strength,
   they shall mount up with wings like eagles,
they shall run and not be weary,
   they shall walk and not faint.

(Isa. 40:27–31)

Chapter 2

Work vs. Fatigue

"Will you walk a little faster?" said a whiting to a
   snail,
"There's a porpoise close behind us, and he's
   treading on my tail."

So writes Lewis Carroll in *Alice in Wonderland.* A whiting is
one kind of fish and a porpoise is another creature that lives in
water. This I learned from my dictionary. But all of us know
that a snail is synonymous with slowness.

This story is a parable of our work: We have to move faster
because we are always behind and something is gaining on us.
Would that we could blame this situation on some slow-
moving person ahead of us. We cannot. We blame it on the
assembly line moving too fast for us to keep up. We blame it
on the unfairness of the competition, the lack of appreciation
from our superiors, the lack of opportunity for advancement,
etc. Whatever we blame it on, we come home at night
exhausted, fatigued. The fatigue is only slightly less when we
arise from our sleep and push ourselves to work the next day.

Maybe if you and I understand our fatigue better, we can
discover springs of renewal in the day's work itself. Maybe we
can get more mileage from the energy we use, with less wear
and tear on our organism. The speed of advanced communi-

cations systems today is that of light—186,000 miles a second, or about two thirds of a billion miles an hour. The speed of transportation possible today—in the case of dozens of kinds of aircraft, chiefly military—is faster than 1,040 miles an hour, the rate at which the earth revolves. In our imagination, you and I often think that we must do our work *that* fast, too! Such expectations make fatigue epidemic.

What Is Fatigue?

Fatigue is weariness from labor or exertion; it is exhaustion of strength. It is your overall response to the demands or stresses placed upon you. These demands and stresses may come from your work situation. They may come from the countless tasks you undertake and from the expectations you have of yourself. Or they may come from the despair you feel about routine activities that demand little or no physical exertion but impose intolerable strain upon your happiness and dignity and frustrate your sense of purpose in life. You would rather be elsewhere, doing something else, or even being someone else!

Fatigue clearly results from overexertion either at work or in athletic activity that is not balanced with rest and restoration of energy. Studies of bodily processes show that during work, oxygen and glucose are consumed. Waste products are formed such as carbon dioxide, exhaled from the lungs, and uric acid, excreted in the urine. In this sense, your fatigue may be measured in terms of a bodily state in which waste products are in high concentration. Your human organism is, then, an energy-converting system with a definite functional relation to work performance. This is a normal process in every healthy person.

However, basic physical and emotional disorders can be

operative in producing fatigue. An underactive thyroid gland may produce a wide range of fatiguing symptoms. Emphysema shortens the breathing capacity of a person, and he or she wears out rapidly. Arthritis and other pain syndromes exhaust a person. Poor nutrition shows up especially in school children who are easily fatigued. Pregnant mothers take nutritional supplements as the fatigue of pregnancy wears them down. Obesity is a vicious cycle of fatigue and eating in its own right. The excessive weight takes *energy* to carry around. The obese person tends to substitute food for rest, and that adds to the weight. Similarly, alcohol can be taken by a fatigued person in order to get a "lift" of temporary good feeling.

The most persistent psychological factor in fatigue and exhaustion is *stress*. Hans Selye described the three phases of stress as alarm reactions, followed by resistance or coping measures, followed by exhaustion. Thomas Holmes outlined forty-three stress events associated with severe losses such as the death of a family member, a divorce, a job loss; or with changes in one's life situation such as changing jobs, sleeping conditions, places of dwelling; or with moving from one era of life to another as when graduating from school, taking one's first job, getting married, becoming a parent, or retiring from work. He suggested that the *accumulation* of these stress events in exceptionally brief spans of time make fatigue and exhaustion more likely. Yet other persons, such as Marc Fried and Peter Bourne, aptly observe that we can raise our capacity for tolerating stress through discipline, skill development, adequate equipment with which to work, and clarified motivation for living and working. Those about us can reduce fatigue and exhaustion when they appreciate our efforts and reward us adequately for them.

A more subtle psychological force in fatigue is the factor of *motivation.* Abraham Maslow is most helpful in relating our motivation for action, effort, and work to a hierarchy (different levels) of needs. The most basic of these are survival instincts and needs such as food, shelter, and sexual gratification. Next comes the need for safety. Higher still are the needs for belonging and love. Next come the needs for self-esteem, self-respect, and personal dignity. At the peak of the hierarchy are the needs for self-actualization and personal achievement. As Robert Frost put it in "The Death of the Hired Man," we need something we can "look backward to with pride" and something we can "look forward to with hope." Without these needs being met, you and I lose heart and develop "giving up and giving in" responses to life's demands, and what energies we have are depleted more quickly. Jesus spoke of this as "fainting with fear and with foreboding of what is coming on the world" (Luke 21:26). In the secular push of the day's work this collapse of morale is dubbed "burnout," a chronic state of being worn out with one's work, a pervasive form of fatigue. Zest in living and working is the opposite of this kind of fatigue.

Rest and Renewal in the Face of Fatigue

You have every right to ask me: "Now that I know what fatigue is, how can I deal with it rather than let it become a way of life that gradually wastes me away?" Let me see if I can make some concrete suggestions to answer this question.

Quit Trying to Live Life All at Once

I mentioned the speeds of communication (186,000 miles a second) and transportation (more than 1,040 miles an hour) that are possible today. As Marshall McLuhan said, the world has become a global village. This atmosphere of our age has

seeped down into our beings in such a way that we expect
instant accomplishment of any task. We expect to live our
whole lives in a moment's time. This is a temptation that tests
our characters even as it did Jesus' character in the wilderness.
"The devil took him up, and showed him all the kingdoms of
the world *in a moment of time,* and said to him, 'To you I will
give all this authority and their glory; for it has been delivered
to me, and I give it to whom I will. If you, then, will worship
me, it shall all be yours' " (Luke 4:5–7). Just like that! Just
like that? In a moment of time? Who is deceiving whom?
Jesus' remarkable grasp of the slow wisdom of the laws of
growth and personal discipline under God would not permit
him either to be deceived or to deceive himself. There are no
shortcuts! There are no quick fixes. Instant achievement is a
false hope that uses you up, wears you out, and fatigues the
very tissues of your body.

To be more specific, take a look at what Thomas Holmes
said about stress events accumulating in *a short span of time.*
Some of these events are *developmental* events. They are
mileposts of maturity. You can burn yourself out by crowding
these events into a short span of time. You may be trying to
finish school, succeed mightily on your first job, get married,
and buy a new car and a new house *all at once.* You do have
some power to spread these events out if you are not
deluding yourself that all these can be yours in a moment of
time.

David Elkind, in his book *The Hurried Child: Growing Up
Too Fast Too Soon* (Addison-Wesley Publishing Co., 1981),
has shown how we push growing sons and daughters into
adult behaviors, denying them the right to grow up gradually.
We want instant adults of our children just as we want instant
achievement for ourselves. This pushiness fatigues the stuff of
our being. By the time children are sixteen they have "seen it

all," and by the time parents are thirty-five to thirty-eight they think of life as having passed them by. Do not allow this telescoping of your life eras by jamming them together; it could wear you out prematurely.

Take an Honest Spiritual Inventory of Your Basic Health

As we have seen, the condition of your health affects your fatigue and energy level. You as a Christian may be like some Christians to whom the apostle Paul wrote in the sixth and twelfth chapters of Romans. You may believe that your body has nothing to do with your spiritual energies and sense of well-being under God. Hence, you may be trying to live your life *as if* you don't *have* a body. You can do as you please and your body will not be bruised, you may think. Not so! This is a second great self-deception.

If you act as if you do not have a body, the first message your body gives you to tell you that you are deceiving yourself is the message of fatigue. You experience fatigue first as a distortion of your perception of things and events around you. Then you begin to make poor decisions and your judgment is impaired. Then you fall into confusion and conflict with yourself and others. A rigorous and honest inventory of your health and health habits is urgent.

For example, here are several questions for you:

1. How many hours of sleep do you think you need to be an efficient person? When I ask people this question I am amazed to hear them say four, five, and six hours more often than seven, eight, or nine, though the latter estimates are more humanly realistic.

2. Do you smoke tobacco or marijuana? If you cut them out, your breathing will provide more oxygen to your whole

body, and especially to your brain. You will head emphysema or lung cancer off at the pass. Your fatigue level will be reduced and your energy level increased.

3. Are you overweight? You may be substituting food for rest and sleep. Are you? Do you use high-calorie food and drink to offset fatigue? If you bring your weight to normal, you will find that this releases fresh energy and that you can move with less effort.

4. Do you get enough physical exercise? Walking or swimming are complete exercises. You may be a jogger or a runner, but you don't have to be an athlete to take seriously walking and patterns of exercise that a good physiotherapist can prescribe. Weave these into your daily routine.

5. Have you seen your doctor lately for an examination and testing that would reveal such energy-depleting processes as hypothyroidism, low blood pressure, anemia, and others that your physician can identify clinically?

Develop a Code of Energy Use

Very few people consciously work out a code of behavior that specifically targets the flaws in personal philosophy that fate them to waste energy, accumulate fatigue, and to get the least return for the maximum investment of their life force. You need not be one of these thoughtless persons. You can "code" your own behavior by some working principles that assure you of an economy of energy, a minimum of fatigue, and a maximum return on the minimum investments of your life force.

Hans Selye, the Canadian physiologist who pioneered the studies of stress, says that most people can break out of being race horse achievers or passive turtle absorbers of stress and fatigue by learning a code of behavior for their use of energy. He suggests three principles for such a code:

1. Decide what your own personal level of stress and fatigue is that is most creative and comfortable for you. It should be as uniquely personal to you as your fingerprints. For example, how much responsibility can you carry at home and work and still be productive and relatively easy to live with? Or, how many hours a day can you work most wisely and still be the most effective worker? This will determine how much overtime you accept. Or, for that matter, do you have a code as to what overtime is?

2. Decide that personal survival is a prerequisite for being of any service to others or to yourself. Selye calls this "altruistic egoism." The best way to survive personally is to build up a "bank" of the goodwill, respect, support, and love of one's neighbor. Selye says that this is "the most efficient way to give vent to pent up energy and to create enjoyable, beautiful, or useful things." (Hans Selye, *The Stress of Life*, rev. ed., p. 452; McGraw-Hill Book Co., 1976.) Another way Selye has of saying this is that you and I are to live by a philosophy of gratitude. Nothing fatigues us worse than to have our best efforts taken for granted. Even the deeply religious person who gives to, or works for, a great cause anonymously does so in secret and enjoys the gratitude of God for having pleased God.

3. Work at sustaining your neighbors' affection. Maintaining their respect, trust, and love builds lasting relationships. They become your life support system and you theirs. You bear one another's burdens and fulfill the law of Christ and the very balances that keep you going. The hymn of Howard A. Walter states this well:

I would be true, for there are those who trust me;
   I would be pure, for there are those who care;
I would be strong, for there is much to suffer;
   I would be brave, for there is much to dare.

I would be friend of all—the foe, the friendless;
   I would be giving, and forget the gift;
I would be humble, for I know my weakness;
   I would look up, and laugh, and love, and lift.

I would be prayerful through each busy moment;
   I would be constantly in touch with God;
I would be tuned to hear the slightest whisper;
   I would have faith to keep the path Christ trod.

It may be that this "coding" does not fit you. Well and good! Then stand back from your fatigue and rethink your priorities. Work out your own code before God. Do not be tossed to and fro by the sea of demands upon your energy. Set your sails and your course so that you rest in your own convictions.

Chapter 3

The Restfulness of the Rhythm of Life

Have you ever noticed that the busiest and most active organ in your body as far as physical exertion is concerned is your heart? It beats 70-75 times a minute, varying somewhat in older and very young persons. This amounts to about 36,000,000 beats a year! Yet you must realize that these beats are always happening on an exertion-rest rhythm. The *rhythm* of the heart is of greatest importance. The heart cycle of rhythm is timed from the end of one heart contraction to the end of the next contraction. The rhythm consists of an exertion and contraction, called the *systole*, and a period of rest, called the *diastole*. In other words, this fearfully and wonderfully made organ *rests* half the time in rhythm with its exertion phase of the other half of the time. This delicate balance is found in the healthy heart.

The work-rest rhythm of the heart is more than just an analogy, a metaphor, or a parable of the very nature of life itself. Concretely and actually it is a working example of the *way* life works, the way we were created. We can ignore and desecrate this basic rhythm of rest and work, and we will pay the price for it in disease, disorder, and misery. Or we can attune ourselves to the inherent rhythm of life and reap the benefits of having driven and maintained ourselves according to the design of the Creator and Ruler of life, the everlasting God. You can find the basic rhythm in your heart's faithful work and rest cycle. You can find it in the rhythm of sleep and waking, and in the cycle of events from birth to death. As you go beyond your own body and life history, you can find the rhythm of life in all creation. You can genuinely sing:

> This is my Father's world, and to my listening ears
> All nature sings, and round me rings
> The music of the spheres.
> This is my Father's world: *I rest me in the thought*
> Of rocks and trees, of skies and seas;
> His hand the wonders wrought.
>
> (Maltbie B. Babcock)

Letting Yourself Catch Up with Your Body

The story is told of a South American tribe that would be on a long march, day after day, when all of a sudden the people would stop, sit down to rest for a while, and then make camp for a couple of days before going farther. They said they were letting their *selves* catch up with their *bodies.* You have, most scientists believe, an intrinsic time clock of rhythms intrinsic in every cell. These rhythms persist under constant conditions. (Charles F. Stroebel, "Chronopsychophysiology," in *Comprehensive Textbook of Psychiatry/II,* Vol. 1, p. 167.) The fact that commercial jet airliners can travel faster than sound does not change but only complicates the intrinsic time clocks you and I have in us. Jet lag exemplifies this. There is a four- to five-day period of fatigue and readjustment needed after a transcontinental or transoceanic flight through several time zones. You can anticipate this by artificially adapting to the time schedule of the place of your destination one week before your departure. Or you can plan stopovers along the way to let your internal rhythm catch up. Or, if your schedule will permit it, you can continue to eat, sleep, work, and play on the time clock of your home location all through a visit to another continent or to the other end of this one. The whole purpose of this adjustment of your rhythm is to be sure that in making critical decisions your judgment will not be impaired by your being out of synchrony within your internal circadian ("circa," around; "dies," day) 24-hour cycle.

Other examples of this rhythm of your being are at every hand. Rhythms underlie what is assumed to be in the range of the constant balance in people and the world. "In health, a human being has an appearance of stability that cloaks an inner symphony of biological rhythms—a spectrum ranging from microseconds for biochemical reactions, milliseconds for unit nerve activity, about a second for the heart rhythm, the 90-minute rapid eye movement cycle of dreaming (while asleep), the major 24-hour rest-activity cycle, the 27-day menstrual cycle, and, finally, the single life-span cycle" (ibid.). Your best opportunity for "laboratory" observation of these rhythms is when, twice a year, most of the nation shifts one hour from standard to daylight saving time. From highly technical studies of the brain, the skin, the urine, the blood, the plasma, and the body as a whole, reasonable conclusions have been drawn at such places as the University of Minnesota chronobiology laboratory. These studies show that our bodies vary cyclically and rhythmically in their ability to tolerate stress, to function at their best, and to detoxify and excrete poisons and drugs. These especially appear in our emotional responses. We can snap to attention fairly quickly at any moment night or day and converse intelligently, abstract, and reason. Yet at the same time, our moods and our capacity for empathy will not be so cooperative. They vary significantly and ritually over a 24-hour period.

An important part of your own serenity and peacefulness in living rests in your getting to know your particular rhythm of life. Are you an A.M. personality, rising early in the morning fully alert and with energy at its peak; and do you find that the hours between 3 P.M. and 6 P.M. are "down times" for you? Or, on the other hand, are you a P.M. personality, one who really does not get going until mid or late morning but becomes a dynamo of energy from 11 P.M. to 2 A.M.?

Your answers to the above questions will give many basic clues as to which shift you work on, which time of day you do your crucial decision-making, and when during the 24-hour cycle you are *more likely* to rest, sleep, "goof off," have a party, etc. Also, the rhythm of your day has to be timed to relate well to the rhythms of those with whom you live. Husbands and wives have a major discipline, especially early in their marriage, in synchronizing their best times with each other and providing solitude for each other in the recuperative times of their lives. When this is ignored and romantic love is falsely taken to mean being with each other at all times and places, real marital trouble is in the making. A specific example is in the rhythm of the sexual life of a couple. We live on a continuum between great spontaneity, on the one hand, and great indifference, on the other. A couple can consciously tune their lives to their mutual times of spontaneity and indifference, using the first for sexual enjoyment, play, and laughter, and the second for separate activity, rest, solitude, and contemplation. Unsatisfactory impasses can occur through self-centeredness and neglect of the building of a mutual rhythm. In these cases, the partners go their own ways and develop parallel lives, each rarely entering the other's world. Isolation sets in and the contractual elements of being legally married begin to feel like shackles from which to be liberated.

The Rest Cycle Within the Wakeful Day

In the early 1950s, Patricia Carrington, Harmon Ephron, and others did research that points "to the existence of roughly 80 to 110 minutes during a waking day when persons are in a reverie, a *day*dream. These moments do not come all at the same time but alternate with periods of outwardly directed thinking of a more practical and logical nature." (Patricia Carrington, *Freedom in Meditation,* p. 139.) Clinical observation demonstrates this. Notice yourself in the middle of your duties at work when you catch yourself staring at the wall or out a window. Note the times during a meeting when you are definitely "out of it." Although the state of consciousness may seem to be boredom, it is not; you may be quite engrossed in what is going on. On the contrary, your whole being of itself cuts out to rest a bit. Notice also the skill of accomplished public speakers who use silences, humorous stories, tender and emotional stories, and other strategies to "rest" their audiences. Also remember how the dentist uses a rhythm of rest and work in repairing your teeth! Watch yourself when you are driving your car, too, when you suddenly jerk to the realization that in your abstraction you have already gone past your destination!

These "rests along the way" are *there* in the flowing process of your being. Why not take advantage of them, use them as times of meditation, imagination, contemplation, and prayer? Bring them into your *deliberate* way of life. Rely upon the rhythm of the wisdom of your body to enable you to be renewed through these times of reverie. I myself am committed to exercising my inalienable right to spend some time each day simply "staring at the wall" or focusing my meditation on a small wooden cross, at the Star of David on my wall, or at one of the several art pieces my students and patients have given me.

In the early years of my ministry, I worked alongside a much older and more experienced pastor. He seemed never to hurry and seemed to enjoy and savor his work. He noted that I did not function this way. He said to me: "You must learn to sit easy in the saddle; the Christian ministry is a long journey!" I have taken him at his word, and having now become as old as he was then, I can affirm his wisdom from years of practice. The rhythms of the resting cycles in a day's waking activity are *put there,* it seems to me, by the all-wise Creator for the constant renewal of our being, for he intends that the journey of life be much longer, healthful, and filled with joy than our 100-yard-dash mentalities will ever permit.

Savoring Each Stage of Your Life Cycle

Your whole life has a predictable rhythm in its seasons. The psalmist comments on the shortness and fragility of our lives, even if we live our threescore and ten, or fourscore, years to the end. Then he prays: "So teach us to number our days that we may get a heart of wisdom" (Ps. 90:12).

That heart of wisdom embraces an awareness that in the order of creation, God "has made everything beautiful in its time"; also he has put eternity in our minds; but even so we "cannot find out what God has done from the beginning to the end" (Eccl. 3:11). Such knowledge is too awesome for us; it is high, we cannot attain to it (Ps. 139:6). Yet the seasons of our own lives we *can* know. We can attune ourselves to their rhythm as surely as we adjust to the seasons of the year— winter, spring, summer, and fall. In this attunement is our rest and our ecstasy in savoring each era of our existence, that of our family around us, and that of the circle of our friends and the larger community. Festival and fasting, rejoicing and mourning, greeting and farewell, arriving and departing, become the pulsating rhythm of emotion at the stages along life's way, at the passages from one era of the life cycle to the other, from birth to death.

Yet for the average American, moving from one stage of life to another is something to be either ignored and denied, hurried through, or anticipated with fear and dread. Hence, we exaggerate into physical symptoms and inappropriate behavior the natural anxiety of growth from one stage of life to another. It is hard for us to put away childish things, quit looking back with nostalgia, and take the leap of faith into the newness of life.

On the contrary, let me suggest that a way of durable rest and renewal of life for you and me is to commit ourselves to savoring each era of our life cycle. Live life to the hilt in each stage along life's way. This savoring of life Walt Whitman called "wondering." To wonder is to be filled with awe at both what can and what cannot be known:

> I do not think seventy years is the time of a man or
> woman,
> Nor that seventy millions of years is the time of a
> man or woman,
> Nor that years will ever stop the existence of me
> or any one else.
> Is it wonderful that I should be immortal? as every
> one is immortal,
> I know it is wonderful ... but my eyesight is
> equally wonderful ... and how I was conceived
> in my mother's womb is equally wonderful,
> And how I was not palpable once but am
> now ... and was born on the last day of May
> 1819 ... and passed from a babe in the creep-
> ing trance of three summers and three winters

to articulate and walk . . . are all equally wonderful.
And that I grew six feet high . . . and that I have
become a man thirty-six years old in
1855 . . . and that I am here anyhow—are all
equally wonderful;
And that my soul embraces you this hour, and we
affect each other without ever seeing each other, and never perhaps to see each other, is every
bit as wonderful.
("Who Learns My Lesson Complete?" from *Walt
Whitman's Leaves of Grass: The First (1855) Edition,* ed. by Malcolm Cowley, pp. 140–141; Vi-
king Press, 1959)

Evelyn Duvall has described stages in family development
and has given the approximate number of years we spend in
each era. She has determined statistically that the average
American couple will spend two years before they have
children, twenty years rearing, educating, and setting free
their children, and then have twenty-five to thirty years of life
before one or the other spouse dies. (Evelyn Millis Duvall,
Marriage and Family Development, 5th ed., p. 148; J. B.
Lippincott Co., 1977.)

The crucial point of this discussion of the life cycle is that
much of our restlessness and fatigue arises from our igno-
rance or unawareness of the normative rhythm for a healthy
and productive person. This in turn prompts us to try to *rush*
through life rather than to pause, to savor, and to wonder
with awe at the strengths for living each era that life has for
us. In other words, we destroy the rhythm of the life cycle
with inordinate haste, false ambition, and lack of discipline.
We fear that life is passing us by when in fact we are passing
life by in our pell-mell rush. For example, I am in the era of
later maturity and I am often tempted to neglect the chances

to be a good grandparent. Yet to intensify my attention, wonder, and savoring of the revelations of my grandchildren makes the past seem to be worth all the effort and the future to be intensely intriguing as I watch the growth of my grandchildren today.

A young couple—as a further example—may not have children yet. They may want to enjoy the awe, wonder, and savoring that comes from getting to know each other more profoundly, from taking advantage of their freedom to travel, and from forming lasting friendships with other couples their age. Little do they realize that they are preparing themselves to be the best of friends and comrades in the later stage of the contracted family, the "empty nest" stage, when all the children are grown and out of the home. When people attend closely to the issues of the intense present, the past and future take care of themselves.

Paul Tillich puts it this way: "Every moment of time reaches into the eternal. It is the eternal that stops the flux of time for us. It is the 'eternal now' which provides for us a temporal 'now.' . . . People who are never aware of this dimension *lose the possibility of resting in the present.* As the letter of Hebrews puts it, they never enter into the divine rest. . . . The eternal rest . . . stops the flux of time and gives us the blessing of the present." (Paul Tillich, *The Eternal Now,* p. 131; Charles Scribner's Sons, 1963. Italics added.) The Moffatt translation of Deut. 29:29 says it best: "The hidden issues of the future are with the Eternal our God, but the unfolded issues of the day are with us and our children for all time."

Chapter 4

The Rest
of
Breathing Easily

When you are really tired, you tend to say: "I am out of breath." When you have been extremely busy, you may say: "I haven't had time to catch my breath." After severe exertion and uninterrupted effort, and when the job is finished, you sigh with a deep breath and say something like: "I'm glad that is over." When you want to interrupt your work and rest awhile, you are likely to say: "I'm going to take a breather." When you are intensely at work and your full attention is on what you are doing, you breathe more shallowly. When you are taking a brisk walk and paying attention to everything in general and to no one thing for very long, you breathe more deeply. When you go to sleep, your breathing drops into a long rhythm of deep breathing. Therefore, the connection between the way you breathe and the way you rest or do not rest is evident at every turn of your day and night.

Yet this gift of breathing is likely to receive little attention, discipline, and appreciation from most of us. Have you noticed what a remarkable function of your very life your breathing is? Let me in this chapter examine with you the way your breathing nurtures, rests, and renews your whole being and suggest some specific disciplines for enlisting your breathing in the resting and renewal of your life.

Breathing and Our Creation

In the earliest account of creation, found in the second chapter of Genesis, we are told: "Then the LORD God formed man of dust from the ground, and breathed into his nostrils the breath of life; and man became a living being" (Gen. 2:7). The King James Version translates "living being" as "living soul." Our word "soul" translates the Hebrew *nephesh* and the Greek *psyche* in the Old and New Testaments respectively. In the Bible, the word "soul" does not (except in rare instances) mean a separate entity from the living, breathing body of the person as it does in Plato, Plotinus, and other Greek philosophers. The word "soul" really means "life" or "living being," the "self" that is capable of hunger, anger, love, and sexual passion, and that has the power to make decisions and to act upon them. More concretely it means "breath of life," as in Gen. 2:7.

The breathing being, as portrayed in the rest of Scripture, always refers to the Creation story for its essential meaning. Let's look at some dramatic examples of this. Job makes elaborate reference to the "breath" of the "breather." In Job 27:3–4 he says: "As long as my breath is in me, and the spirit of God is in my nostrils; my lips will not speak falsehood, and my tongue will not utter deceit." Then again in Job 33:4 he says: "The spirit of God has made me, and the breath of the Almighty gives me life." In Job 34:14, the intimate relationship of breathing to life versus death is clear: "If [God] should take back his spirit to himself, and gather to himself his breath, all flesh would perish together, and man would return to dust." Isaiah teaches the same thoughts as Job: "Thus says God, the LORD, who created the heavens and stretched them out, who spread forth the earth and what comes from it, who gives breath to the people upon it and spirit to those who walk in it: 'I am the Lord, I have called you in righteousness, I have taken you by the hand and kept you; I have given you as a covenant to the people, a light to the nations, to open the eyes that are blind, to bring out the prisoners from the dungeon, from the prison those who sit in darkness' " (Isa. 42:5–7).

Here Isaiah not only describes the gift of breath in God's creation of us; he also gives the reason or purpose of our breathing—to open the eyes of the blind, to set persons at liberty, and to bring light to those who sit in darkness. In brief, you and I breathe more easily when we have a clear sense of purpose and are sure of our reason for being and breathing. I recall vividly a professor of mine at Wake Forest College who, in a gently humorous way when he met me on campus, would say: "Wayne, I want you to tell me in two or three sentences what you are doing today to justify the good Lord's wisdom when he gives you the air you breathe!" With laughter of good friends together, I would try to answer his challenge.

In the New Testament, the remarkable parallel to the Creation story is the gift of the Holy Spirit by the resurrected Christ:

> On the evening of that day, the first day of the week, the doors being shut where the disciples were, for fear of the Jews, Jesus came and stood among them and said to them, "Peace be with you." When he had said this, he showed them his hands and his side. Then the disciples were glad when they saw the Lord. Jesus said to them again, "Peace be with you. As the Father has sent me, even so I send you." And when he had said this, *he breathed on them,* and said to them, "Receive the Holy Spirit." (John 20:19–22, italics added)

In the New Testament the word for "soul" is *psyche,* which comes from the verb form meaning "to breathe." It refers to the "life" or "vitality" of a person. God cares for our life (Matt. 6:30); our life can be saved or lost (Mark 8:35); and our life can be laid down (John 10:11). Our life can be sorrowful, even unto death (Mark 14:34); our life can magnify the Lord (Luke 1:46); our life can be troubled (John 12:27); and we can be anxious about our life (Matt. 6:25). In these last senses, the life or the soul is the very stuff of our emotional beings. Predominant among these emotions is that of fear or anxiety.

The apostle Paul uses a word for the soul or the spirit that you and I read in our English Bible as "body." He uses the word "body" to refer to the total person. Shakespeare and the translators of the King James Version of the Bible used the word "body" in the same sense. I can recall my grandmother, who taught me to talk as an infant, referring to herself and any other person as "a body" in the way the lyric does: "When a body meets a body coming through the rye." In a sentence, you do not say, I *have* a body, but, I *am* a body. In this perspective the apostle Paul says: "I appeal to you therefore, brethren, by the mercies of God, to present your bodies as a living sacrifice, holy and acceptable to God, which is your spiritual worship" (Rom. 12:1).

You do a spiritual service when you present your very breathing body to God as a temple of the Holy Spirit in response to Jesus Christ's having breathed upon us and urged us to receive the Holy Spirit. What is the practical meaning of this?

The Function of Breathing in Your Body

All that has been said thus far means that the "breath of life" in your body is a spiritual force, the agent of your consecration to God. Therefore, you can profit by a practical knowledge of how your breathing works in your body, because you take your body seriously. How is it related to your rest and restlessness?

Respiration, or breathing, is the process by which sufficient oxygen for the needs of body cells is supplied to them and by which most of the waste carbon dioxide is eliminated into the atmosphere. The air is pumped by the lungs, chest, and abdomen. Minute air sacs in the lungs provide a surface for the exchange of oxygen and carbon dioxide. The blood transports oxygen and carbon dioxide as it is pumped by the heart. All organs of the body are thus sustained. However, your brain, which constitutes only 2.5 percent of your body weight, receives 15 percent of the output of blood from the heart and uses 25 percent of the blood oxygen in the process. The brain can tolerate only a 10 to 20 percent drop in its oxygen supply without causing an undersupply or no supply of oxygen (hypoxia or anoxia). Your *total* function mentally, physically, and spiritually, your very life, then, depends upon regular, complete, and healthy oxygen supply in your blood to your brain. The words of Leviticus 17:11 and 14 are literally true: "For the life of the flesh is in the blood. . . . The life of every creature is the blood of it."

The practical question then is: What increases and enhances that life, and what destroys it?

Clean Air or Polluted Air

I went on an emergency call to the hospital where I work. A family had called me upon the death of the father, a 45-year-old man. He had died of emphysema, a disease in which the air sacs in the lungs are clogged or otherwise unable to exchange the oxygen and carbon dioxide. The man's brain had suffered such a loss of oxygen that on three occasions in the last five years of his life he had become severely mentally ill as a result. Finally, the disease killed him.

As I became better acquainted with his life story from his wife and children, I learned two very important facts. First, he had worked all his life in the dust and dirt of a large cement factory. Second, he had since his youth been a heavy smoker. The pollution of the air he breathed was directly related to the disease that racked his restless body with coughing, kept his brain from functioning, and finally killed him.

You can add to your ease of breathing, to the restfulness of your sleep, and to your total well-being mentally and physically by doing everything possible to clean up the air you breathe. You will think more clearly, make better decisions, and be a more serene person if you do not use tobacco or marijuana. If you do use either or both, then determine to break the habit as a way of "presenting" your body unto God. You will not break these habits without much encouragement and support from your family and friends. Ask for it. You will not do so without help from the Power that is greater than yourself. Ask for that help.

Furthermore, examine your living and working conditions and change them to the extent of your ability. If you must live and work in dust, fumes, and smog, then use filter masks, air conditioning, or even supplemental oxygen to offset their effects. Be a part of campaigns for clean air and water in your community. If you get a chance to move and choose the place to go, then include clean air and water in the factors that determine your choice.

Hope or Depression

Rarely do we associate the level of our hopes with the quality of our breathing. In Venice there is a bridge that led from the medieval courtroom to the prison. It is called the

Bridge of Sighs. We do sigh when we are fatigued, exhausted, grieved, nostalgic, or depressed. A sigh is a deep, prolonged, and audible inspiration and expiration of air. You usually sigh involuntarily. Life begins to slow down for you and spontaneity slips from you. Your energy level is at a minimum. Your thought processes bog down and your interest in persons, things, and events dulls. Life becomes tedious and tasteless. Your outlook becomes hopeless. You are tired.

You might imagine that this is *all* mental or *all* spiritual (because you can't seem to think, and because you feel worthless). You might imagine that it is *all* physical (because you have a feeling of being choked up and beset by physical symptoms). None of these possibilities alone is the case. Your whole being is involved and your mental abilities, your capacity to perceive, and your bodily functions are intricately bound together. In mild depressions, you can deliberately take physical exercise, increase your heart rate, increase the depth and regularity of your breathing. Doing these with another person will inspire (breathe into) your efforts. If this does not suffice, then you need to see your doctor because he or she knows the kinds of changes that are going on in your blood chemistry. By now you may have become uncharacteristically sleepy or sleepless. The doctor can help you regulate this by medical means whereby your appetite, level of energy, and sleep routine can be improved. Buried under all this sighing is an indignation, an impatience, a feeling of injustice, even as Jesus experienced it when he found a man who was deaf and had a speech impediment. Mark 7:34 tells us that, "looking up to heaven, he sighed and said to the man, 'Be opened.' " His sighing was one of indignation that the man was suffering. Down under your sadness is some indignation and even rage. Talk these feelings through with a trusted confidant such as your physician or your pastor. Pour out your complaints in prayer to God for guidance. Then you will breathe more easily and the tide of life will return with fresh energy, new reasons for hope, and a calmer and more natural rest when you sleep. Depression is a part of your alarm system. It is a painful suffering that lets you know that rest and renewal are no longer an option but an inescapable necessity. Pay attention to its message and give yourself some breathing time and space. You are a conscientious person and have earned the right to rest and renewal.

Security or Fear (Anxiety)

If depression is the great lion that knocks the breath out of you and destroys your rest, then fear, or anxiety, is the thousand mice that shorten your breath and cramp and restrict your chest, lungs, and stomach with fear, anxiety, or insecurity. The main fears that we struggle with are the fear of abandonment by those we love; the fear of separation both from those we love and from the job or other security upon which we rely; the fear of making a wrong decision; the fear of change; the fear of the condemnation of our own conscience; and the fear of losing control and becoming helpless. Some would say that underlying all of these fears is the one great fear of death itself. I agree with this. Robert Browning said it in his *Prospice,* written after the death of his wife, when he called death the "Arch Fear."

If you are breathing the restless breath of your fears, I have no way of divining or putting my finger on *what* your fear is. However, let me suggest an exercise for you. Here is a list of the fears I have named above. On a sheet of paper, write your answers to the following questions, giving specific events, memories, or things you face with dread. This will make it easier for you to turn my generalities into *your* specifics:

1. The fear of being abandoned by whom?
2. The fear of separation: (*a*) From whom? (*b*) From what?
3. The fear of making a wrong decision about what?
4. The fear of change: (*a*) From what? (*b*) To what?
5. The fear of condemnation from your own conscience: (*a*) About something you have already done? (*b*) About something you are being tempted to do?
6. The fear of losing control: (*a*) Over whom? (*b*) Over what?
7. The fear of becoming helpless in what way?
8. The fear of death?

Now ask yourself how well grounded in fact your fears are. We have realistic threats around us much of the time. In this age of psychological self-analyzing, we deny ourselves the right to be honestly afraid of what does and should scare anyone, and thus we avoid responsibility for taking well-planned precautions against the threats to our own best interests. Separate these fears from your groundless fears. These groundless fears arise from within your own thinking, from old scary messages that you remember ever so vaguely from past experiences, and from your need for presence and affection from those on whom you have learned to depend, maybe too much for your own good.

In any event, the fears—grounded or ungrounded—still provoke the same tenseness, breathlessness, and constriction of your lungs, chest, and abdomen. Fear is like electricity. If it is *not* grounded, it is not really dangerous to your safety and security. If it *is* grounded, it is very dangerous. In *both* instances fear is terrifying! Some of the same physiological and psychological costs tend to be exacted. Let me propose that Christian meditation is a way of release from these effects.

Christian Meditation

Christian meditation is both different from and very much like other forms of meditation about which you hear and read. Christian meditation is different in that it begins with prayer to God in the name and spirit of Jesus Christ our Lord. Here is an example:

> O God, who did breathe into me the breath of life in your creation of me and who in Jesus Christ did redeem me and breathe upon me as he gave me the Holy Spirit, I thank you for the air that I breathe, the nostrils, lungs, chest, and abdomen with which you enable me to breathe, and the blood that courses through my arteries and veins to the minutest part of my being. Enable me now to exercise and use these gifts to the fullest, that I may present my whole being to you as a spiritual offering. Through Jesus Christ, whom I love and whom I serve, I pray. Amen.

Now, the simplest way of exercising and using God's gift of breathing is as follows:

1. Sit erect in a firm, straight-backed chair, close your eyes, and place your hands gently on your thighs. Begin to be aware of your breathing. Relax and breathe naturally. Breathe primarily from your abdomen. Focus your attention on the movement of air through your nostrils, down your windpipe into your lungs, into your abdomen, and back out through the same amazing set of organs. Breathe in and out normally five times.

2. Breathe in to the fullest extent possible and say: "I am . . ." Then breathe out just as completely and say: "Relaxed."

Do this five times quite deliberately and purposefully.

3. Do this same exercise but add to it your own *image* of the nostrils as the air passes through them, your windpipe, your lungs, and your stomach. Reverse the pictures in your mind as you breathe out. Do this five times.

4. Now return to your normal breathing pattern and pray a prayer of thanksgiving for the nourishment of your blood, the interchange of oxygen and carbon dioxide in your lungs, the nourishment of your heart and brain by the oxygen, the quickening of your mind, and the privilege of fellowship with God.

5. Finally, enjoy the quietness and rest that have come to you in this experience of breathing. Cast all your anxieties upon the Lord, for he cares for you. Resolve to live today to the fullest and let the future take care of itself. Shift to living life twenty-four hours at a time.

Chapter 5

Sleep:
The Knitter
of Raveled Spirits

Shakespeare gave us a dramatic picture of the most important force for rest in our lives:

> Sleep that knits up the ravell'd sleave of care,
> The death of each day's life, sore labour's bath,
> Balm of hurt minds, great nature's second course,
> Chief nourisher in life's feast.
>
> *(Macbeth II, ii, 36)*

In the previous chapter we saw how depression and anxiety almost by definition are thieves of normal sleep. Sleep is the "knitter" of the spirit raveled out by anxiety, the balm of the mind hurting with indecision, hopelessness, deep indignation, and unspent anger. These, as Shakespeare said of Glamis in *Macbeth*, have "murder'd sleep." Your right to rest is the assurance that these things need not be. Obstacles to your nightly entering into the rest given to you by God, the Inventor of sleep, can be removed and you can claim God's blessing of sleep as your own. In this chapter, let us reflect upon what sleep is, how it works, what it does for us, and how we can enter into its rest.

The Nature and Function of Sleep

Normal sleep is the natural, almost complete cessation of consciousness, during which the activity of the nervous system is almost suspended and the powers of the nervous system are revitalized, rejuvenated, and refreshed. You will notice I have used the word "almost" twice in the previous sentence. We speak of sleeping "the sleep of the dead," but in fact our sleep is never the *complete* cessation of all our functions that death represents. In fact, anxiety about death may *keep* us from sleeping, for fear that we will not awake. The little child's prayer that begins, "Now I lay me down to sleep," also has a line in it, "If I should die before I wake . . ." We take this line for granted, but should seriously question whether teaching little children to associate sleep with death is at all wise. I would rather teach my grandchildren to pray:

> Thank you, God, for the gift of sleep.
> Help me to rest and make me new.
> All my loved ones safely keep,
> And tomorrow we will be loving you.

When you sleep, you go through four stages of rest, in which there are two kinds or qualities of sleep. In the 1950s, researchers in the physiology of sleep, using the electroencephalogram to chart the activity of the brain during sleep, noted that one kind of sleep is "rapid eye movement" or "REM" sleep. This is an active or activated sleep during which the images you see in your dreams apparently are "seen" and actively watched while you sleep. They also recorded a second kind of sleep, the "*non* rapid eye movement" or "NREM" kind, when you are in a quiet, deep, inactive sleep.

These two kinds of sleep alternate with each other, both appearing in each of four 90-minute stages of sleep. This 90-minute REM-NREM sleep is a part of a basic rest-activity cycle in your 24-hour day. (Even when awake, you alternate on an 80-100 minute cycle of first an outwardly directed practical and logical kind of thinking, and second an inwardly directed daydreaming, reverie, or meditative kind of thinking.) The total sleep cycle consists of 20-25 percent REM sleep and 75-80 percent NREM sleep.

Sleep need varies with age: 16 hours are needed at birth, 15 hours at four weeks, 14 hours at twenty-six weeks, 12 hours plus an hour nap at two to three years, 11 hours plus an hour nap at four to five years, 10 hours at eight to twelve years, 9 hours at twelve to seventeen years. Adults need 8 hours, and elderly persons average significantly less because of frequent awakenings. Yet in the elderly, frequent naps make it difficult to assess their sleep time. My own feeling is that if older persons miss sleep at night, a deliberately planned "siesta," i.e., a nap in the afternoon, will keep them invigorated and recuperated with a good average of 7 to 8 hours sleep. Thus their youth is renewed. Where older people err is in assuming that they are fated to get less sleep and that their work schedule should be the *same* as that of persons in their thirties to fifties. Not so. Periodic shifts in the pattern of the day's work, punctuated by "dropping out of sight and sleeping," will enable us to be productive and creative *differently in time* but in a way that is *qualitatively* satisfying nevertheless.

Effects of Sleep Loss

Obvious Effects

Experimental studies show that total sleep loss creates both dramatic and incapacitating changes in how people act and think. False or pseudo-psychotic states *can* result, as was seen in prisoners of war under torture: feelings of persecution, misperception, confusion of time, place, and personal identity, and hallucinations of seeing and touching. These changes occur after about 100 hours of total sleep loss. The marvel and miracle is to see all these changes disappear once persons recover their sleep. They quickly reconstitute, and no pathological effects extend beyond the period of the sleep deprivation.

Subtle Effects

Less dramatic effects appear in your life, however, when you are heavily but not totally deprived of sleep. Your judgment is poor, you tend to "lose your grip" on your emotions, and your decisions become faulty. You may do and say some unwise things that in themselves may have permanent effects, not upon your brain, but upon your job, your marriage, your sons and daughters, and your friends and co-workers. You may make unwise financial and business decisions that have lasting effects. Therefore, the consistent pattern of not acting on major decisions until you have had a chance to "sleep on them" is a ritual worthy of all acceptance.

The Work Situation

Persons caring for seriously ill family members, especially mothers and fathers of little children and grown sons and daughters of aging parents who require twenty-four-hour nursing care (which is amazingly expensive to buy), are likely to suffer profound sleep deprivation. Likewise, persons in heavily responsible jobs may be repeatedly pushed into "forced marches" of forty-eight-hour to ninety-six-hour stints of work without sleep. Management and labor in heavy industry, physicians and nurses in understaffed situations of health care, and farmers in times of threatened destruction of their crops are just a few examples of persons for whom a sleepless existence can become a way of life. If you are in a situation such as I have described or in any other that is similar, then you need a systematic plan for interrupting your stress, getting someone else to "cover" for you on the job, and regularly taking what military personnel in Vietnam called "R and R's," periods of rest and recuperation. This is imperative *now*. Rotating in and out of the severe work schedule for "sack time," for rest, food, and loving care, is your inalienable right, your right to rest. Furthermore, your efficiency on the job may be low as a result of your lack of rest. Think about this. Defiance of the basic needs of your body for sleep can reach the point where you are defying the Creator, who made your body. You think *you* know better than God does! Oh, no!

Unsatisfactory Substitutes for Sleep

In depriving yourself of sleep, you will become so fatigued that you will fall back on a variety of unsatisfactory substitutes for rest. Take an inventory of your practices with me.

Caffeine. The most available stimulant you can find to pick you up, give you a lift, and make you more active is caffeine. It is a stimulant. Caffeine is usually consumed in the form of coffee, tea, cola drinks, and chocolate. Often, for example, parents will say that their child is hyperactive, when in fact he or she has been drinking numerous cola drinks in a day's time. The child *may* not be sleeping. You as an adult, carrying a burden of fatigue, can speed yourself up with more and more coffee, tea, cola drinks and chocolate in its multiple forms. Cut this out or cut it down to an absolute minimum and you will feel the need for rest sooner and be more likely to sleep well when you lie down.

Food. All things are lawful, but not all things are fitting. Food is certainly O.K. However, when you become so fatigued you can't push yourself any more, you may combine calories with the caffeine. Pastries, chocolates, snack or junk foods such as potato chips, french fries, and a long list of others you can name, along with soft drinks, alcohol, and hors d'oeuvres, are substitutes for rest in the middle of the morning, afternoon, and evening. They are supposed to refresh you and give you quick energy. You take on from 500 to 1,000 calories in these socially convivial occasions, breaks, and rat-race pit stops in your day's work. Hence, the connection between fatigue and overweight is a double one: you eat to combat fatigue; your excess weight fatigues you all the more. The rebound effect is a self-perpetuating circle of fatigue. Simple rest and preferably adequate sleep break the cycle.

Alcohol. Some people find that alcohol pushes them beyond the fatigue barrier with an initial feeling of well-being. This becomes a substitute for rest and sleep. Sooner or later it may become a substitute for food as well. Paradoxically enough, alcohol is also used by some people as a sedative *in order* to sleep. It is an unprescribed drug that is not a stimulant like caffeine, but a depressant. In the short run, it may seem to erase fatigue or facilitate sleep. Alcohol, just as caffeine and food, has its ceremonial, celebrative, preservative, and even therapeutic uses. I do not mean to negate it as the part of creation that it is. The one thing I want you to hear me say here is that neither alcohol, food, nor anything else is a substitute for sleep.

Sleep is like air, water, and food, a necessity to your body. There are no substitutes for these things. They recuperate, renew, and sustain your body. They are agents of health that only you can safeguard for yourself. When it comes to sleep, especially, do not take any substitutes. Demand and take the real thing.

Going to Sleep and Remaining Asleep

You may have trouble going to sleep and staying asleep until your customary rising time. Several normal obstacles cause this most often.

Grief

If you have lost someone or something extremely important to you, you will have trouble sleeping. This is to be expected. You may lose a lover or a spouse by a broken courtship or a divorce. You may lose a coveted promotion or your job itself. The best way to handle these griefs is to "talk out" your thoughts and feelings in the daytime, during waking hours, with a trusted friend, a trained counselor such as the pastor of your church, or a pastoral counselor on the staff of a hospital or community pastoral counseling service. Similarly, members of your family can talk things out with you and bring an intimate comfort to you. Yet if you live alone, you may need to have a close friend or relative stay with you until you are able to sleep the whole night through. The "long night watches" can be very lonely. You don't need sympathy that is too sweet and makes you feel helpless. You need understanding from someone who will let you say exactly how you feel and find real sense in it. (For a detailed discussion of grief, read my book *Your Particular Grief;* Westminster Press, 1981.)

Indecision

A second deterrent to sound sleep is indecision. You stay awake trying to figure out problems. Your mind is up in the air. You can't go to sleep because you can't settle what you are going to say to someone tomorrow, because you are second-guessing what you did or said the day before this night, or because you do not know enough facts about a given situation to make a good decision. Thus, instead of sleeping you toss and turn as you stew in indecision. You can do something about this. Let me suggest a few things.

First, you may need specific information which you do not have now, and without which you cannot decide what to do. However, you *can* decide *how, where,* and *from whom* you can get that information. Do that. If you are afraid you will forget these details, get up and write yourself a note including all of the details about information needed and ways and means of getting it. Go back to bed and you are likely to go to sleep.

Second, you may know that nothing can be decided or done *now* about what is worrying you. At this time, you are in a "holding pattern." (In flying with commercial airlines, I have never been able to sleep while a plane circled in a holding pattern for up to an hour waiting for a *time* to land.) By analogy, you will have trouble sleeping out of sheer suspense. Yet in the ordinary course of human events, you can decide *when* you can put an end to the suspense of *how long* you intend to put up with the unsettled state of affairs. Once you have set an *end* beyond which you do not have to go, or beyond which you will not go, you will tend to rest more easily and sleep more readily. You will begin to relax, both when awake and when asleep.

Third, you can develop alternatives for action. In your indecision, you cannot sleep well because you are confused. Clearly defining alternatives is the best way to resolve the confusion, as surely as the sun burns off the early morning fog. Confusion cannot stand the heat of clarity. As you define the alternatives, possible actions you can take and the predictable results of each of these actions, you can rank them in order of your preference as Plan A, Plan B, Plan C, etc. If you are already in bed and cannot go to sleep, then you can reach for a light, a pen, and a pad and write these alternatives down. Then you can sleep with a more settled mind.

All that I have said here points to something missing in our daytime activities when we cannot sleep. We need significant times alone and in contemplation about decisions that need to be thought through and nailed down. If your life is like mine, hectic and event-filled, then you may again and again be denied the luxury of a period of time for solitude, meditation, and reflective decision-making. However, if you and I nevertheless pull back, stand apart, and turn aside from the hectic, pell-mell rush of the demands upon us, we restore our perspective and do not let life demand this time of reflection out of our sleep time. We will sleep more serenely. Procrastination about overdue decisions comes at the price of sleeplessness. Therefore, as much as you can, make decisions within a day or two after the choices present themselves. Research the facts, inspect the alternatives, bite the bullet, and get on with it.

A charming example of this is found in the exquisite story of Ruth in the Bible. Boaz and Ruth wanted to get married. However, Jewish law said that her deceased husband's next of kin had first option on marrying her. Perplexed, Ruth went to her mother-in-law, Naomi, who seemed to know Boaz better than Ruth did. Naomi said: "Wait, my daughter, until you learn how the matter turns out, for the man will not rest, but will settle the matter today." Boaz did just that and removed the roadblocks in the way of his having Ruth for his wife. I find myself wanting to copy the character trait of Boaz wherein he would not rest but would "settle the matter today."

Yet Jesus reminds us that we are not to respond on our own cleverness in deciding what to say. In the intense trials that Jesus' disciples faced before authoritarian rulers of their day, Jesus told them: "Settle it therefore in your minds, not to meditate beforehand how to answer; for I will give you a mouth and wisdom, which none of your adversaries will be able to withstand or contradict" (Luke 21:14–15). You and I are not alone in settling decisions in our minds. We have a Spirit within our spirits that is more than our spirits. We can count rest in the assurances of Ps. 121:1–4: "I lift up my eyes to the hills. From whence does my help come? My help comes from the LORD, who made heaven and earth. He will not let your foot be moved, he who keeps you will not slumber. Behold, he who keeps Israel will neither slumber nor sleep."

Pain and Sleep

One of the most real disrupters of your sleep is or will be physical pain. You may have a cold or the flu, and during its brief course (which seems forever) congestion in your head and chest will interrupt your sleep. You may be beset by a more continuous pain such as that of arthritis or the residue of old injuries. Instead of causing transient pain, this condition and many others like it become chronically painful disorders. By their very nature, they tend to carry with them a chronic sleep disorder. When pain persistently interferes with your sleep, you need careful, conservative medical diagnosis, treatment, and instruction. Many physicians will blandly tell you that "you are going to have to learn to live with the pain." However, either they do not know how to teach you to live with it, or they are in too big a hurry to do so. Therefore, let me suggest that you go to the kind of physicians who not only are skilled in diagnosis and treatment but also, along with their therapy, will teach you how to be a part of your own pain management. Usually these physicians will be physiatrists, who specialize in physical medicine and rehabilitation, or neurologists, who specialize in nonsurgical treatment of the disorders of the central nervous system. Their treatment aims to help you *avoid* as much surgery as possible. Their treatment will be comprehensive and conservative. Follow their advice as to whether you need the assistance of a surgically skilled person such as a neurosurgeon or an orthopedist.

Quite apart from relying too heavily on the hope that surgery will completely "fix" your pain, your more common hope will be that some sort of medication will solve your pain. If your physician places you on any kind of medication, follow these guidelines:

1. Be sure to advise your physician of the *other* medications that other physicians may have you taking. This will reduce the possibility of one medication conflicting with another, creating a hazard or rendering neither medication effective.

2. Have yourself checked at least once every three months to see whether the medicine is still needed, is still effective, or should be changed or discontinued.

3. Whether it is pain-relieving or sleep-inducing, be very skeptical of staying on any medication regularly over long periods of time. Medication should be reserved for acute crises of pain.

Far better than medicines or surgery is to make the changes in your life habits that will reduce your stress, increase your use of carefully prescribed exercise, well-planned rest, and adequate sleep. Medicines, particularly, should be short-term aids in making these life-style changes. Throughout our country today, hospitals and other health facilities are providing what are called wellness centers, life-style centers, or health awareness centers. These can provide excellent guidance in pain control, weight control, and stress control. Seek out one of these centers and get a comprehensive approach to your life pattern in coping with pain.

Sleep, Meditation, and Prayer

Relaxation, meditation, and prayer have been the centuries-old ways of assistance for getting to sleep. Let me recommend Herbert Benson's *The Relaxation Response* or Patricia Carrington's *Freedom in Meditation*. These will give detailed instructions that the limited pages of this book will not permit.

In a distinctly Christian approach, your first resource is the Scriptures, especially the Psalms, especially Ps. 3:5–6; 4:8; 121:4; and 139:17–18. Proverbs 3:21–24 will be a sustaining grace: "Keep sound wisdom and discretion; let them not escape from your sight, and they will be life for your soul and adornment for your neck. Then you will walk on your way securely and your foot will not stumble. If you sit down, you will not be afraid; when you lie down, your sleep will be sweet." Other references in Proverbs tend to add words of caution about overvaluing sleep, such as Prov. 20:13: "Love not sleep, lest you come to poverty; open your eyes, and you will have plenty of bread." A similar observation is found in Prov. 24:33–34: "A little sleep, a little slumber, a little folding of the hands to rest, and poverty will come upon you like a robber, and want like an armed man."

This latter admonition, which concentrates on the connection between laziness and poverty, nevertheless, also points to the hazard of being obsessed with the necessity of sleep. You and I can easily become worshipers or idolaters of the Greek god Morpheus, the god of sleep and dreams. Even with sleep, we are wise to keep ourselves from idols, as I John 5:21 urges us. If you find that after trying too hard to sleep you cannot sleep, then get up and read, listen to music, or engage in some other task you really enjoy. Sleep will take care of itself. It may be as simple as that you are not tired enough to sleep yet!

However, another resource for encouraging sleep is prayer. If you cannot sleep, use the available quiet time to devote yourself to prayer. Instead of being agitated and worried about problems and people, systematically lift them and yourself to God in prayer. You will undergo some deep personal changes in yourself, even as Jacob did when he wrestled all night until the break of day (Gen. 32:22–32). He was no longer the same after this night in which he said: "I have seen God face to face, and yet my life is preserved." Your relationship to God is more important than one night's sleep.

Yet one of the major differences between God and us is that we are made to rest as well as work, to sleep as well as be awake. God stays awake and watches over us and this world we know about, as well as all those worlds we do not know

about at all. Hence, we can with a good conscience pray for
sleep. The following prayer for sleep and rest says it for us:

> Eternal God, the God and Father of our Lord
> Jesus Christ, the central peace and the source of
> all rest in the universe, I thank you for the
> permission you give me to rest in you, free of
> despair, fear, distrust, and indecision. You bless
> me in taking all my burdens upon yourself, that I
> may sleep according to the way you have intended
> to renew my being through sleep. Deepen my
> breathing, that I may have each cell of my body
> replenished with oxygen. Relax my muscles, that I
> may be healed of my fatigue. Teach my overactive
> thoughts to be still and know that you, and not
> they, are God.
>
> In my sleep, command my dreams that they may
> be agents of your healing of my thought processes,
> instruments by which you reveal your intentions
> for my life. Grant that my very sleep may be that
> deeper communion with you.
>
> Then, as I awake, may I face the day ahead of
> me with hope, anticipation, and full commitment
> to love you with all my heart and my neighbor as
> myself. Through Jesus Christ our Lord I pray.
>   Amen.

Chapter 6

The Restless and the Greedy

During World War II, I was the pastor of a church in my home city of Louisville. I was asked by a member of the church to visit one of his relatives who was a patient at a large tuberculosis sanatorium. When I arrived at the man's bedside, I found him to be a personable and talkative man of about forty years of age. I asked him how he felt about being in the hospital for such a long stay. He responded: "I am being paid back for my sin." I did not quickly move to reassure him. Rather, I asked him: "Your sin? What did you do?" Immediately he responded: "I wanted it all, Reverend." I asked: "What do you mean when you say you wanted it all?" He said: "Well, you know how scarce labor is with all the able-bodied men in the war. I got me a job at 'the powder plant' [a munitions factory in our area], and they wanted me to work all the shifts I was willing and able to work. You know the pay is the best I ever made. I wanted it all. I would work three days three shifts without sleeping. Many days I would work two shifts. I was so greedy that I broke my health down and landed in here. That was my sin. The Lord made me lie down."

We talked about his healing process and how the very conditions of healing were a form of God's forgiveness and

God's instruction of him in a discipline of his desires to what
is really important. What does it profit a person "to gain the
whole world and forfeit his [or her] life"? (Mark 8:36).

This honest man was one of the very few persons I have
ever heard confess the sin of greed or covetousness. Two
stories from the ministry of Jesus present contrasting examples of how greediness requires our very lives of us and, on
the other hand, how peace and serene rest of spirit *can*
happen to us when we are changed by the Spirit and invitation
of Jesus Christ.

The first story is that of the rich fool:

> One of the multitude said to him, "Teacher, bid
> my brother divide the inheritance with me." But
> he said to him, "Man, who made me a judge or
> divider over you?" And he said to them, "Take
> heed, and beware of all covetousness; for a man's
> life does not consist in the abundance of his
> possessions." And he told them a parable, saying,
> "The land of a rich man brought forth plentifully;
> and he thought to himself, 'What shall I do, for I
> have nowhere to store my crops?' And he said, 'I
> will do this: I will pull down my barns, and build
> larger ones; and there I will store all my grain and
> my goods. And I will say to my soul, Soul, you
> have ample goods laid up for many years; take
> your ease, eat, drink, be merry.' But God said to
> him, 'Fool! This night your soul is required of
> you; and the things you have prepared, whose will
> they be?' So is he who lays up treasure for
> himself, and is not rich toward God." (Luke
> 12:13–21)

Here the man's fantasy was that if he simply enlarged his
investments, increased his holdings, and laid up ample goods
for many years, this would bring ease. This ease would be one
he would *take,* as contrasted to the promise of Jesus in Matt.

11:28 that if we take his yoke upon us, he will *give* us that
same ease, that rest which we are trusting "much goods" to
provide us. The very act of wrongly placing our trust can
require of us our life, because greed consumes *us*. Its
voracious appetite is cannibalistic.

The second story is that of Zacchaeus:

> He entered Jericho and was passing through. And
> there was a man named Zacchaeus; he was a chief
> tax collector, and rich. And he sought to see who
> Jesus was, but could not, on account of the crowd,
> because he was small of stature. So he ran on
> ahead and climbed up into a sycamore tree to see
> him, for he was to pass that way. And when Jesus
> came to the place, he looked up and said to him,
> "Zacchaeus, make haste and come down; for I
> must stay at your house today." So he made haste
> and came down, and received him joyfully. And
> when they saw it they all murmured, "He has gone
> in to be the guest of a man who is a sinner." And
> Zacchaeus stood and said to the Lord, "Behold,
> Lord, the half of my goods I give to the poor; and
> if I have defrauded any one of anything, I restore
> it fourfold." And Jesus said to him, "Today salva-
> tion has come to this house, since he also is a son
> of Abraham. For the Son of man came to seek and
> to save the lost." (Luke 19:1–10)

Zacchaeus had amassed a fortune through his despised task
as a tax collector. In coming face-to-face with God in Jesus
Christ, he was radically transformed in his attitude toward
both his power and his possessions. When Jesus asked to be
his guest at his house, he was overwhelmed by the calm
forgiveness dramatized in this request. He received Jesus
joyfully and announced: "Behold, Lord, the half of my goods
I give to the poor; and if I have defrauded any one of
anything, I restore it fourfold." Jesus assured him that

salvation had come to him and his house. The *gift* of rest and ease of heart became his. He could be freed of the burdens of greed by sharing with the poor. He could be freed of the burden of injustices he had committed by making restitution fourfold to those whom he had wronged. His life was not required of him because of his greed; rather, it was restored to him as he found the Lord Jesus Christ at the center of his loyalties, the controlling force of his behavior.

Kinds of Greed

Greed is not always for or about the same objects of desire. Yet it is one of the reasons most often given for not resting, for being fatigued. However, persons giving the reasons usually are unaware that greed is the source of their restlessness. "Gaining" is the verb that corresponds to the actions of greed. We struggle against poverty so hard and with enough success that the *process* of gaining money and property becomes an addictive fascination in itself. We gain prestige when we become financially successful; then the power over others associated with money makes money a means to the greed for power and control. We build a certain concept of ourselves as always being in control, "calling the shots," "naming the tune" for others to dance by, and this ego state itself must be fed more and more. Thus the maintenance of a certain image, or ego, becomes a form of greed. Even in the sphere of religious leadership, we may be so greedy for recognition and adulation that we are threatened, restless, and strained when someone else steps into our spotlight. The many-hued spectrum of greed reveals itself upon refraction to be far more than the yen for money and property. Yet we can agree with Virgil, who said: "Curst greed of gold, what crimes thy power has caused." Whatever the *kind* of greed, all kinds have one thing in common: the appetite of greedy persons is insatiable and leaves them as restless after gaining things as they would be thirsty after drinking seawater.

Loneliness and Greed

A part of this restlessness is the inevitable by-product of the main mechanism of greed—inordinate, compulsive competitiveness. Competitiveness of this kind leads, not to the camaraderie of teamwork, but to isolation and loneliness. Fyodor Dostoevsky speaks of the subtle connection between greed and loneliness, restlessness and genuine security:

> All mankind in our age have split up into units, they all keep apart, each in his own groove; each one holds aloof, hides himself and hides what he has, from the rest, and he ends by being repelled by others and repelling them. He heaps up riches by himself and thinks, "how strong I am now and how secure," and in his madness he does not understand that the more he heaps up, the more he sinks into self-destructive impotence. (Fyodor Dostoevsky, *The Brothers Karamazov*, tr. by Constance Garnett, p. 363; Random House, Modern Library, n.d.)

Dostoevsky describes vividly what Philip Slater calls our American "pursuit of loneliness." In the pursuit of affluence, prestige, and power, we paint ourselves into corners of quiet personal desperation and loneliness. We perceive others, he says, "as an impediment, or a nuisance: making the highway crowded when we are rushing somewhere, cluttering or littering the beach or park or wood, pushing in front of us at the supermarket, taking the last parking place, polluting our air and water, building a highway through our home, and so on." (Philip Slater, *The Pursuit of Loneliness,* p. 8; Beacon Press, 1970.)

Such encounters as Slater describes are filled with strain, stress, feverish hostility, and even rage. Rest, tranquillity, and renewal are the antithesis. In all our getting we have gotten neither rest nor peace.

Excess Baggage and Fatigue

The end result of the day-to-day existence of greed-ridden persons is to be weighed down with and worn down by the excess baggage of things and power they have collected. Their lives become cluttered with more than they can use, more than they need or want. The mere accumulation of things, houses, land, and money becomes an energy-consuming force in its own right. In a sense, "all these things" begin to develop a life of their own. If you are such a person, they control *you* and you are not in control of your own life. Ecclesiastes 3:5 says that there is "a time to cast away stones, and a time to gather stones together." Maybe you have already gone through your time to gather stones together and it is time, as was true of Zacchaeus, to cast away stones. In Heb. 12:1 the faithful Christian is urged to "lay aside every weight, and sin which clings so closely" in order to run with perseverance the race that is set before us. This is not a race to get the most, to get it all, to get there ahead of everyone else, to have the last word, to hush everybody else. No. This is a collaborative race in fellowship with other Christians. We compete with each other only in doing honor to one another and in loving our neighbor as ourselves because we love God.

Such a perspective will help us get a fresh angle of vision on what is most important in life. Those whose greed makes them unhappy unless they are $100,000-a-year persons may be working sixteen hours a day, seven days a week, putting in 112 hours a week. Even at the baseline of a 50-hour week, this is working more than two shifts! Such persons are not $100,000-a-year persons but $50,000-a-year persons who work two shifts! I have seen patients come into our hospital exhausted, depressed, and having made some very unwise decisions. In one case the patient had worked 183 days without a day off. Those were fourteen- to sixteen-hour days.

Similarly, I have counseled married couples in which both partners worked such hours. Their relationship to each other suffered enormously. Efforts at intervening in this system of work were very difficult. Yet the concerns that brought them in for counseling were not about their relationship to each other but about the behavior of adolescent sons or daughters. I am not suggesting that we go back to the old "submission" system of the wife not working. I am suggesting that lowering the standard of living, creating more quality time together, and spending money on family events rather than bigger houses, more clubs, more and finer automobiles, etc., would make better use of the resources of life. You will not rest unless you create time for rest and for peaceful communion with your family. Even if you do gradually start blocking out time for yourself with your family, at first you will be anxious and feel at a loss as to what to do with yourself. You will have to break through that wall of anxiety to rest peacefully.

The Simplification of Life

You have a right to rest without selling that birthright for all of the excess baggage that you are accumulating. The liberation of your life to rest in the way God created you lies within your own power if you will discipline your desires and distinguish between what you really need and *what you think*

other people expect you to have, not even necessarily what you
yourself genuinely want. Mencius, in the fourth century B.C.,
in his Oriental wisdom said: "To nourish the heart there is
nothing but to make the desires few." You and I have much
more time to replenish and recuperate our total beings if we
learn (get someone to teach and encourage us, if necessary) to
get along, as Zacchaeus did, with half the stuff we have and
feel we must have in order to be a person. As Richard E.
Byrd, the Antarctic explorer, said in his account of a journey:
"I am learning . . . that a man can live profoundly without
masses of things."

A Living Example of Simplification

One remarkable example has been set for older persons in
the simplification of life by some young people. I know a
large number of them who have simplified their lives drasti-
cally as contrasted with us as their parents. As married
couples, they share in the preparation of meals. They plant
and cultivate a garden. They make Christmas gifts by hand,
applying arts and crafts they have learned and learned well.
Out of sheer curiosity, they have learned several skills. Their
clothing is appropriate but simple, casual, and comfortable.
They are as likely to ride a bicycle to work as to drive a car.
Increasing numbers of them, if married, are managing as a
one-car instead of a two-car family. When they go on
vacations their main solution of their need for housing is to
camp or to stay with friends along the way. They tend to
enjoy hiking, swimming, searching for food at the seaside, in
streams, or in meadows and woodlands, where wild plants and
berries can be found. If they do buy food, they usually
prepare and cook it themselves over a campfire or stove.

Frankly, I admire their simplicity and the functional ways
they have of making life pull their families and their friends

together into a community rather than apart in isolation. As Dostoevsky again says: "True security is to be found in social solidarity rather than in isolated individual effort" (*The Brothers Karamazov*, p. 363). These younger persons reflect the wisdom of our elder son, Bill, when in 1959 we moved from a smaller house with one bath into a larger one with two baths. He had been uprooted from his friendship group in "the old neighborhood," as he called it. He was eleven and his chums meant much to him. He said: "I would rather have two friends than two baths!"

Some Simplification Disciplines

Cultivating Inner Serenity Instead of "Other-Directedness." Many years ago David Riesman, with others, wrote a book entitled *The Lonely Crowd* (Yale University Press, 1950). In it he spoke of the "inner-directed," who have a heritage of a clear sense of direction in life and who live according to self-chosen goals. He contrasted such persons with the "other-directed," those whose contemporaries or peers provide their sense of direction. Other-directed persons shift direction and change goals as they are swayed by the media and friends. In being exceptionally sensitive to the wishes and actions of others, they find life becoming increasingly complex. You can readily see that to be too literal about Riesman's different types of persons can become absurd. You do not want to be sensitive to doing things to please everybody with whom you come into contact. Yet you do not want to be self-centered and inconsiderate of everyone but yourself. This reduces the insight to absurdity.

This is not what Riesman, or I, would want to convey. Rather, my point is that your life becomes more simplified if you draw on the inexhaustible riches of the mind and teachings of Christ for your sense of direction in life rather than on the fads, fashions, and total approval of the style setters around you. No greed is quite as subtle and yet as all-consuming as the greed for everybody's approval. A reverse form of this is the greed for everybody's *disapproval*—both are other-directed. You and I will simplify our lives, what we do, how we do it, what we buy, wear, eat, drive, and enjoy when we are guided by the inner wisdom and balance of an austerity and simplicity we draw from Jesus of Nazareth. Our lives become complex when we are consumed by our greed for being like everybody else, following the latest advertising hype, and living life in hourly awareness of being conspicuously in the spotlight of other people's expectations.

Facing Rather than Retreating from Loneliness. I have spoken, and quoted Dostoevsky, about how greed isolates. Loneliness produces restlessness. Loneliness is another thief of sleep. You may escape loneliness by fretfully working more, making more money, buying more things. In your loneliness you may assuage the pain by going on a buying spree. Then you are in debt and you punish yourself for your extravagance by working more and resting less. Overwork is one way of running from your loneliness.

To simplify your life, turn and face your loneliness for what it is. Arnold Toynbee said that he was a confessed work addict and that the source of his work addiction was his fear of loneliness.

Carl Sandburg spoke most eloquently of loneliness in an interview with Ralph McGill in 1966. He and McGill were walking about Glassy Mountain, near Sandburg's home. He said to McGill: "I often walk here to be alone. Loneliness is an essential part of a man's life and sometimes he must seek it out. I sit here and I look out at the silent hills and I say, 'Who are you, Carl? Where are you going? What about yourself, Carl?' You know, one of the biggest jobs a person has is to learn how to live with loneliness. Too many persons allow loneliness to take them over. It is necessary to have within oneself the ability to use loneliness. Time is the coin of life. You spend it. Do not let others spend it for you."

When you keep pushing more and more work into the lonely spots of your life, you are ordinarily letting others spend time for you. Do it yourself and quit running from your loneliness. The rest you get will be healing.

Learning How to Get Along Without Things. My mother was an uneducated woman who worked in cotton mills from the time she was ten until she was seventy-two. She taught herself to read, write, and count, and she learned the oral tradition her mother—my grandmother—gave her and later gave me. She lived to be ninety-one years of age. Upon our visits back home, I was always impressed by the simplicity and ingenuity with which she lived. She could have done even better at it if she had not by brute poverty been forced into a life-long habit of borrowing money. She did this out of habit long after there was any necessity for it. Occasionally on my visits, I would suggest that I buy something for her that would make life more comfortable or pleasant. She refused, saying: "I'm all right. *I'm used to doing without such things.*" She could say with the apostle Paul: "I have learned to find resources in myself whatever the circumstances. I know what it is to be brought low, and I know what it is to have plenty. I have been thoroughly initiated into the human lot with all its ups and downs—fullness, plenty, hunger, and want. I have strength for anything through him who gives me power" (Phil. 4:11b–13a, NEB).

A good sense of humor about the vanity of greed taking away our rest and churning our spirits with restlessness is an antidote to the toxic powers of greed.

This wisdom brings back to me the story of our friend Portie Tipton. My wife and I spent a night in his home as his guests. About nine o'clock in the evening, as we sat before the open fire, he suddenly said: "Dr. Oates, are you and Mrs. Oates feeling well?" We both said that we felt quite well. He said: "Well, good. I'm not going to sit up with you. I'm going to bed. I only sit up with sick people!" Then he added: "If there is anything you can see that you need, it is yours. If you can't find what you need, call us and we will help you look for it. If we don't have it, we can teach you how to get along without it." Yet for you and me this is easier to say than to do.

We could have more time for leisure and the enrichment of life if we had someone to teach and encourage us to get along without half the stuff we think we need. But then we would have to learn how to use that leisure.

Chapter 7

Home:
The Place to Be,
to Rest,
and to Leave

Your restlessness may be bubbling up from the deep knowledge that you really have no *place* that is your own home in which to rest. You have no place where you can just be. And deeper than this, you may feel yourself a stranger and a wanderer upon the earth because at the outset of your life you were—and maybe still are—unwanted. Those whom ordinarily you could have expected to welcome you continue to give off messages of "Don't be." (Mary Goulding and Robert Goulding, *Changing Lives Through Redecision Therapy*, p. 39; Brunner/Mazel, 1979.) Your right to rest has been stalemated by the withholding of your right to exist, the warm sense of welcome that having a home in this world means to those who genuinely are loved, received, and celebrated when they come back to their home place. You may feel as did Thomas Wolfe when he spoke of himself as a man who "wanders across the face of the earth and has no home and is an exile." (*The Letters of Thomas Wolfe*, ed. by Elizabeth Nowell, p. 371; Charles Scribner's Sons, 1956.)

Whereas your feeling that your being an exile, without a home, may come from not being wanted from the outset, it may also come from the fact that you yourself have rejected the way of life of your family of origin. You have chosen

goals, behaviors, values, and concerns that are alien to theirs.
Even in terms of your particular faith in God in Christ, you
may, through education, travel, and new experiences of faith,
become, as Ephesians puts it, a stranger and a sojourner,
alienated from your childhood faith and family. Your spirit, as
a result, is restless and placeless, not being "at home"
anywhere. You have the "character of *never dwelling anywhere,*" as Martin Heidegger put it (*Being and Time,* p. 217;
Harper & Row, 1962). A counselee with whom I conversed
put it this way: "I wonder how long it will be before I am
where I am." Often, when persons shed their traditional
beliefs, a vacuum of belief takes place. At best, they tend to
shift from this, to that, or to the other belief. A pervasive
sense of not belonging causes the mind and the heart to pace
restlessly back and forth out of step with each other. This
pacing is a search for a nest, a niche, a place, and a people.
Coming to rest involves these intensely necessary aspects of
living.

On Being Without a Nest

Jesus experienced this homelessness. John 1:11 tells us that
"he came to his own home, and his own people received him
not." His early followers said a little too glibly: "Teacher, I
will follow you wherever you go." He cautioned them: "Foxes
have holes, and birds of the air have nests; but the Son of man
has nowhere to lay his head." He had to stay on the move
because Herod was as eager for his head as he had been for
John the Baptist's. The gracious respite of Martha's, Mary's,
and Lazarus' home seems to have been to him a place where
he could rest.

In the ordinary course of life today, you may be a young
husband or wife. You and your spouse have been in school

and in transit from one school to another for all of your married life. I see people like yourselves among law students, theological students, medical students, and residents of every medical specialty. You may have moved ten or twelve times in the six or eight years you have been married. You may not want to have children until you can settle down somewhere, "build a nest," and be able to relax and rest, knowing that you will not be moving for a while. In fact, you may be eager to have children and cannot; yet no medically definable reason exists to prevent it. The very tentativeness of your work and home situation keeps you tense, "up in the air," and restless. Once you can be more at rest in your mind as to *where* you can be for a predictable length of time, then you become more "ready" to be parents. You will be more likely to be able to have children. Birds' nests are for mating and birthing. People mate and birth best with a nest.

Yet the nest is not forever. The creative part of our restlessness comes out of raising a family to the point that the nest is no longer needed for the young. You see a metaphor of this in Deuteronomy:

> [The LORD] found [Jacob] in a desert land,
>   and in the howling waste of the wilderness;
> he encircled him, he cared for him,
>   he kept him as the apple of his eye.
> Like an eagle that stirs up its nest,
>   that flutters over its young,
> spreading out its wings, catching them,
>   bearing them on its pinions . . .
>   (Deut. 32:10–11)

God cares for the young. A part of it is to "stir up the nest," to push the young out on their own wings, to catch them if they falter or are in danger, yet to keep them leaving the nest.

Paul Tournier, in his book *A Place for You,* says that the essential rhythm of a healthy life is that of "finding a place and leaving a place." We find one place and grow to the limits it permits and then seek another place. Yet this rhythm is only alternately restful. In what ways can you find "a rest" that sustains you, both in the place of the nest and in the unknownness of the leaving of the nest? Where is the continuity?

On Resting in Your Calling

One of the sources of that rest abides in your sense of purpose or calling in life. Jesus' overwhelming sense of mission sustained him in his sense of being unwelcome in the world. It was his overriding concern that brought continuity in his homelessness and serenity in the face of the unknown. He knew *why* he was where he was, no matter where he was. As John 13:3 puts it, "he knew that the Father had put all things in his hands, and that he had come from God and was going to God."

In quite an "unreligious" atmosphere I saw something of the power of a sense of calling to give a continuing sense of place in the world. One of my college classmates, Eugene Brissey, wanted to be a journalist. The professor of journalism at our school chided him and said: "What makes you think you can ever be a journalist?" Brissey replied: "Because I will starve rather than make my living any other way." The professor said: "You will be a good journalist!" From then until Brissey died a premature death from war wounds long after World War II was over, he was a journalist. That was his niche. He moved all over the world, but this calling was his particular cloud by day and pillar of fire by night. It was the inner source of his serenity. He knew from whence he came and where he was going.

Henlee Barnette has wisely said: "Every Christian is called

to . . . minister regardless of how he earns his daily bread. Whether work-related or church-related, the Christian is to remain faithful to the calling of God" (*Has God Called You?* p. 128; Broadman Press, 1959). You may be tempted to confuse prominence, notoriety, and advanced education with the sense of calling. You may suppose that, inasmuch as you are a private person and not one of the eggheads of this world, you need not rest the whole case of your life in a specific sense of calling. On the contrary! Charles Reade was right when he said: "Not a day passes over the earth, but men and women of no note do great deeds, speak great words, and suffer noble sorrows" (*The Cloister and the Hearth,* Chapter 1). Therefore, qualify your own mind before God to think fairly about the end to which you were born, and the cause for which you came into the world. Then settle it in your mind with quiet resolve to give yourself to that. "That" may still be a fantasy, a dream, an architect's drawing in your private mind. Dare to take these fantasies, dreams, and drawings seriously. Develop a plan for turning them into reality. One of the things I like to do with students and counselees is to get them to put into words the answer to the following question: If God granted you to have three wishes fulfilled, what would you most want? I am impressed by the way people speak of these inner strivings as "silly," "impossible," "funny," or "wild." Yet they become serious and say: "I have *always* wanted . . ." Do not let conscience make a coward of you and thereby prevent you from ever acting upon your best aspirations and fulfilling your calling.

Another way of making your own sense of calling vivid to yourself is to ask yourself: "What am I most dogged and persistent about over the pull of the years of my life?" I have seen farmers whose dogged persistence was revealed in their sense of pride that they could raise everything they eat—

except salt and coffee—on their farm. Their inner rest and
serenity showed in their eyes, resonant breathing, relaxed
necks, and unclenched hands as they asked me to let them
show me over their farm. I have seen industrial workers
whose sense of calling surfaced in their commitment as a
labor steward and as an artisan at their task in the factory. It
showed even more transparently in that they saw themselves
as fathers and mothers with a deep hunger for their children's
education, growth, and happiness. Even more universal than
this was the indignation and offense they express when I seek
to pay them for some act of kindness they show me, such as
recharging my car battery when my car dies from a bad
alternator in front of their house, or when they mow my lawn
for me when I am ill. They have, in great numbers, a
persistent mission to be a good neighbor. In turn, I know that
when I serve them, I need to do so as returning a kindness.
The blue-collar world is a barter world of kind acts, and the
government's attempts to estimate the gross national product
and to levy taxes on labor are amusing, when the whole of this
tradition of American labor is known.

What has the matter of calling to do with rest? Just this.
The situations I have described of journalists, farmers, parents, and blue-collar industrial workers all have one thing in
common: they are cameos of inner serenity, chosen satisfac-
tions, and minds at rest within themselves. When you have
found your "niche" in life, it becomes a haven of rest, a source
of security, and a freedom from restlessness to you. It
becomes to you as the orbits of stars and planets are to them,
a destiny, not a fate or doom. Your sense of destiny provides
you with an inner serenity that no one can take from you but
yourself. The poet Wordsworth clearly says it:

> Whether we be young or old,
> Our destiny, our being's heart and home,

Is with infinitude, and only there;
With hope it is, hope that can never die,
Effort, and expectation, and desire,
And something evermore about to be.
                                        (*The Prelude* VI, 603)

God's Action in Being Home to Us

Our search for a lasting home and freedom from exile in the world turns to frustration if we make either our parental home, our marriage and parenthood, or our day's work the *central* source of our resting assured of tranquillity, serenity, and peace. God intends more for us.

In speaking to us at his departure, Jesus gave us a promise of a lasting home here and now. He was not, I am persuaded, talking about the life after death but a living participation here and now. In John 14:23 he said: "If a man loves me, he will keep my word, and my Father will love him, and we will come to him and make our home with him." Here he is describing the family of God in which God is our Father, Jesus is our elder Brother, and the Holy Spirit is our life, breathed into us by the love of Christ. All men and women everywhere are our kinspersons either by creation or redemption or both. The mystical union with God in Christ as our home makes us, not strangers and exiles on the earth, but citizens of the world eager to activate our kinship with people of all races, creeds, cultures, conditions, and shades of difference. You and I need not be orphans in this world. Jesus promised us that he would not leave us orphans in this world. Jesus promised us that he would not leave us orphans (John 14:18, Jerusalem Bible). In the worldwide family of God in Christ, we are never away from home, both in terms of others who believe in him and in terms of our mystical union and

companionship with him. We can genuinely pray as did Isaac
Watts:

> O God, our help in ages past,
>   Our hope for years to come,
> Our shelter from the stormy blast,
>   And our eternal home.

In this we can rest.

Chapter 8

The Prayer of Rest

Augustine, in the first chapter of his *Confessions,* says to God: "Man, this part of creation, wishes to praise you. You arouse him to take joy in praising you, for you have made us for yourself, and our heart is restless until it rests in you." (*The Confessions of St. Augustine,* tr. by John K. Ryan, p. 43.)

In Luke 23:50–56, we find a startling story of the contrast between intense, stressful, heartbreaking work, on the one hand, and rest on the other hand. Jesus had been crucified. Pilate released his body to Joseph of Arimathea, who took it down from the cross, wrapped it in a linen shroud, and laid Jesus in a rock-hewn tomb. It was "the day of Preparation." That was the day *before* the Sabbath. People spent the whole day preparing food and suspending business affairs to avoid all risk of infraction of the Sabbath, which began at sunset. On this occasion the Sabbath was about to begin. The women who had come with Jesus from Galilee "followed, and saw the tomb, and how his body was laid; then they returned, and prepared spices and ointments" with which to anoint his body. This was their heavy day of work, on the day of Preparation.

Then the Scripture tells us: "On the sabbath they rested according to the commandment." The Greek word for rest

used here is *hesychazein*. It means to be quiet, to rest, to
remain silent. They did this. They did not talk or try to figure
out all these monstrous events. They prayed without ceasing.
The kind of prayer in which you do not talk nor try to think
things out for yourself—even before God—has throughout
history come to be known as the prayer of the hesychast, that
is, the prayer of rest. As Henri J. M. Nouwen describes it:
"This rest, however, has little to do with the absence of
conflict or pain. It is a rest in God in the midst of a very
intense daily struggle." He says that this prayer of rest is more
than and different from speaking with God or thinking about
God. The limits of words and logical inquiry are beginning to
be felt by many Christians, although Sundays at church are
filled with speeches and explanations of just about everything, even those severe mysteries for which there are no
words or explanations. The apostle Paul described this wordless groping experience of the prayer of rest in Romans 8:

> Likewise the Spirit helps us in our weakness; for
> we do not know how to pray as we ought, but the
> Spirit himself intercedes for us with sighs too deep
> for words. And he who searches the hearts of men
> knows what is the mind of the Spirit, because the
> Spirit intercedes for the saints according to the
> will of God. (Rom. 8:26–27)

As Nouwen again says: "The prayer of rest is standing in
the presence of God with the mind in the heart; that is, at the
point of our being where there are no divisions or distinctions
and where we are totally one." He quotes Theophan the
Recluse: "To pray is to descend with the mind into the heart,
and there to stand before the face of the Lord, ever present,
all-seeing, within you." Then Nouwen says: "The prayer of
the heart is a prayer that does not allow us to limit our
relationship to God to interesting words and pious emo-

tions." (Henri J. M. Nouwen, *The Way of the Heart*, pp. 54, 59, 61.)

This is the secret of the prayer of rest: it is wordless and pushes past the logical thought processes into the depths of your feelings. You are face-to-face with God, who enables you to *feel* your feelings before you dash into thoughts about your feelings or words to describe them. You do not try to justify God's ways or to explain them to yourself or to that imaginary set of faces of other people to whom you speak more often than to God.

What kind of character do you become when you enter into the prayer of rest?

The Power to Wait and the Prayer of Rest

When you sink your words and contending logic into the prayer of rest in the living presence of God and just let yourself *be* in the presence of God, a whole new perspective of time encompasses you. That which you were in such a hurry to see come to pass fades into insignificance. Waiting is a cardinal feature of the prayer of rest. You walk in a park or a shopping center. You see a young mother sitting, waiting, and watching as her child wanders from her and runs back to her. In between times you catch an inwardly distant look on her face. She is *saying* nothing to anyone. She seems not to be *thinking* about anything. Yet she seems happy, and a sort of peace pervades her face as her hands rest quietly in her lap. Have you captured an external view of a person praying the prayer of rest? Only God could tell you. Only God knows.

Or something has come up in your life that is an insult, an affront, an injustice. You are seething with rage. To act upon your rage now would be action saturated with bad judgment, the height of foolishness. Yet you are filled with impatience.

Visualize what this may be in your day, week, month, or year.
Turn to Luke 9:51–56 and you will find two kindred spirits in
James and John, the "sons of thunder," as Jesus called them.
The people of some nameless Samaritan village had refused
to let Jesus stay in their town because he was on his way to
Jerusalem. James and John were as filled with rage as you are.
They asked Jesus: "Lord, do you want us to bid fire come
down from heaven and consume them?" After all, Elijah had
done that in his day. But Jesus saw another way, warned
them, and advised that they go to another village. It was
neither the time not the place for such "overkill." He himself
could be indignant, angry, and impatient. Yet he urged his
disciples to wait.

Such waiting pushes you past words; all you can do is groan,
snort, spit, and pace. It pushes you down past logic and clear
thinking. In such a state, you are submerged in your heart.
You are ready for the prayer of rest. Back off, stand apart,
focus your whole being on the presence of God. Enjoy God's
presence. Wait before God.

> For God alone my soul waits in silence,
>   for my hope is from him.
> He only is my rock and my salvation,
>   my fortress; I shall not be shaken.
> On God rests my deliverance and my honor;
>   my mighty rock, my refuge is God.
> Trust in him at all times, O people;
>   pour out your heart before him;
> God is a refuge for us.
>
>   (Ps. 62:5–8)

Now you come forth from the prayer of rest with a fresh
perspective of the slights and hurts you have sustained. They
still matter, but they do not matter totally, not even primarily.
You have been given self-control by the prayer of rest. Yet

this was not the *purpose* of the prayer of rest. The purpose of the prayer of rest is to glorify God and to enjoy him forever. The natural side effect of such an experience of waiting before God is to place the transient, fleeting hurts of life in the context of the Eternal. A pimple on the face of life ceases to be a cancer to you!

The Power to Forgive and the Prayer of Rest

When you do not feel forgiven by other human beings or by God, you are bound to them by your need for forgiveness, acceptance, and restoration to their good graces. When *you* can't forgive other persons or God, you have hold of them in that you "hold them responsible," you blame them and cannot be gracious to them. Being held captive in these ways uses large amounts of energy. You carry a load that needs loosing. In fact, such a lack of forgiveness or of power to forgive can exercise demonic power over you and me. People can rightly ask: "What on earth has got hold of you?" The prayer of rest is your way of the heart in this dilemma.

The sense of condemnation by others and by God, or the grinding preoccupation of a grudge of unforgiveness (or both), may have pushed you below the level of words and beyond the limits of logic. Wordy or logical attempts to talk or think your way through and out of them no longer work. You are, nevertheless, by the negative forces that have hold of you, prepared to enter the prayer of rest before God. When you and I, unveiled, face the glory of God in the face of Jesus Christ, several profound changes will take place if we will lay aside all words and arguments and just *be* in God's loving presence.

We find that the bonds of the condemnation we have felt

both from God and from ourselves begin to loosen. The Holy Spirit brings back to us Jesus' words—not ours:

> Judge not, and you will not be judged; condemn not, and you will not be condemned; forgive, and you will be forgiven; give, and it will be given to you; good measure, pressed down, shaken together, running over, will be put into your lap. For the measure you give will be the measure you get back. (Luke 6:37–38)

Jesus' word "forgive" here is rich with such meanings as loosen, set free, release, pardon. It has the image of your and my being in debt and having our debt canceled or pardoned; or, if someone is held in debt to us, blamed by us, it means our pardoning them or canceling their debt. This is the first change that comes over us in the prayer of rest.

Then comes the awesome gift of God's inspiring in us a power to let go of our unforgiveness toward others, of God's letting go of our sins toward those who have wronged us. Turn now to Jesus' parable of the king and his servants, found in Matt. 18:23–35. The parable tells of a king who forgave the debts of his servants according to the way they forgave each other's debts. We are required to forgive our brother or sister in our hearts. Jesus' word "forgive" here has the central meaning of "let off." Strangely enough, "let off," has come back into our common speech today with this same meaning. Two children wrestling on the floor are playing until one gets an unbreakable hold on the other and brings pain to the other. Then the hurting one yells: "Let off!" Grown-ups, too, want to get unbreakable holds on each other, to have the humiliating last word in an argument, to get the best of each other. What a restless, exhausting, painful way to be.

The wisdom of God in Christ comes to us in the prayer of rest: "Let off!" Life is short. Death is sure. Your energy is precious. Rest from this hammerlock you think you have on your neighbor. Cease to phrase in your mind that clever and cutting comment you *wish* you had said the last time you contended with your neighbor or that you *plan* to say the next time you see him or her. Let it go! Let off! In the dark night of sleeplessness in which these rehearsals of your own unforgiveness plague you, return to the simplicity and sincerity of your inmost heart. You might pray Augustine's prayer: "*Noverim te, noverim me*"—"May I know you; may I know myself!" You begin to feel the rest that comes from having received from God the power to forgive and to be forgiven by God. What a rest!

Forgiveness that comes through the prayer of rest brings another realization from a face-to-face meeting with God in Christ. Forgiveness is more than just setting us free or letting go of us as we do the same for our neighbor. The prayer of rest brings to us the tender friendship of God in all God's graciousness. Jesus said that we are to forgive "seventy times seven," which to me means that we do not bestow forgiveness just once and cease to be bothered with it thereafter. Rather, we rehearse that first forgiveness again and again until forgiveness is the habitual atmosphere of our being. Forgiveness is like washing a garment. After you wear it for a while, the garment needs washing again. So too, as time goes on, people need forgiving again.

Forgiveness in this last sense is "being gracious to" one another because we have received the graciousness of God. The apostle Paul said:

> Do not grieve the Holy Spirit of God, in whom you were sealed for the day of redemption. Let all bitterness and wrath and anger and clamor and slander be put away from you, with all malice, and be kind to one another, tenderhearted, forgiving

one another, as God in Christ forgave you.
(Eph. 4:30–32)

"Forgiving one another" here means "being gracious." From the same root spring such words as thanks, gratitude, a gift freely and graciously given, a favor bestowed. Forgiveness is unmerited, unearned. It is a gift. It takes no price, exacts no ransom, and demands no contract. It springs from a greatness of heart, a graciousness of being on your part. You are tired, fatigued, and exhausted by hauling the burden of unforgiveness around with you. Having been face-to-face with God in the prayer of rest, you have laid this burden down. You rest in the graciousness of God's forgiveness.

In turn, you are taking on the character of the graciousness of God yourself. As you behold the glory of the Lord "with unveiled face," you are being "changed into his likeness from one degree of glory to another; for this comes from the Lord who is the Spirit" (II Cor. 3:18). You are, in the prayer of rest, delivered of your burden of unforgiveness and unforgivingness. Remember John Bunyan's pilgrim at the cross and sepulcher (grave) of Christ: "Just as Christian came up with the cross, his burden loosed from off his shoulders, and fell from off his back, and began to tumble, and so continued to do till it came to the mouth of the sepulchre, where it fell in, and I saw it no more." (*The Pilgrim's Progress,* p. 38; Peter Pauper Press, n.d.) The spirit of graciousness springs from gratitude for deliverance. The change in our very being is brought about by the "habitual vision" of the greatness of God, which happens at the heart of the prayer of rest. Thus you and I lay hold of the greatness of heart God has for us, much as Sidney Lanier wrote in reflecting upon the greatness of the sea marshes:

By so many roots as the marsh-grass sends in the
    sod,
I will heartily lay me a-hold on the greatness of
    God.

                (From "The Marshes of Glynn")

Chapter 9

Rest:
The Gift of God
in Christ

You and I were created with the need for rest. "The LORD is the everlasting God, the Creator of the ends of the earth. He does not faint or grow weary" (Isa. 40:28). Yet the Creation story tells us that after God saw everything he had made, and that it was good, and after the heavens and the earth were made, "God finished his work which he had done, and he rested on the seventh day from all his work which he had done" (Gen. 2:2). In God's very nature and in the way God made you and me, then, rest is the gift of life brought to us as we finish acts of creation, whether they be creative work or creative play. Both work and play are energy consumers. They deplete us. Renewal is necessary. Rest renews.

I recall tenderly an event in the first year of my marriage. Since I had been a bachelor until I was twenty-five and worked full-time since I was thirteen, work was second nature to me. Rest did not seem to be necessary. Play was a vague entity apart from the fun of working. One evening when I came home for dinner my wife, Pauline, gently asked me: "Wayne, don't you ever *finish* working?" The thought had not occurred to me.

Yet God *finished* his work and saw that it was good. He rested after finishing the task. I doubt that this means that

God created a closed-end universe. He would always be the God who acts. Jeremiah and others speak of God thus: "The Lord GOD of hosts has a work to do" (Jer. 50:25). Ninian Smart speaks of "the two locations of God." Thus "God's creative activity is not confined to his being there at the moment of creation; but he is present at the continuous creation of the world every day and every minute working thus in all things. . . . Inasmuch as God is a dynamic being, his presence means work, and his being present everywhere thus means that he is working everywhere." (Quoted in Geoffrey Wainwright, *Doxology: The Praise of God in Worship, Doctrine, and Life,* pp. 81–82; Oxford University Press, 1980.)

Jesus confirmed this in his ministry. Upon seeing the man blind from birth, he said: "We must work the works of him who sent me, while it is day; night comes, when no one can work" (John 9:4).

Pauline's question went to the heart of the matter: We never finish absolutely any significant work. Nevertheless, we become exhausted, fatigued, and depleted. We *cease* to work. We interrupt our efforts. We begin to rest. To do so is a part of the rhythm of the creative process. For example, the heart never ceases its work, but paradoxically, in its measured rhythm, it rests half the time! Pauline has been to me that lifelong haven of rest, blessed interruption of stress, and liberator from my compulsive resistance to rest. Hence, she is a continual source of renewal to me. She keeps me in touch with God's gift of rest and renewal.

This gift of rest is bestowed on the living by a God who is the God of the living and not the dead. In three places in the Scriptures rest is referred to as final, as death. In Job 3:17–19, death is referred to as the rest where the wicked cease from troubling, the weary are at rest, the prisoners are at ease together, and the slave is free from his master. If we were to

translate these into goals for living and not solutions presented by death alone, then the great social justice inherent in the
substance of rest would appear. The wicked would cease their
troubling; the weary be at rest, prisoners at ease together, and
slaves set free!

Rest as the finality of death appears again in Ecclesiasticus:
"Weep less bitterly for the dead, for he has attained rest; but
the life of the fool is worse than death" (Ecclus. 22:11). Also:
"Death is better than a miserable life, and eternal rest than
chronic sickness" (30:17).

Yet these are no biblical commendations of death as the
gift of rest. On the contrary, they express the conventional
wisdom that unending, unremitting, and unchangeable depletion of life is worse than death. In comparison to that, death is
rest.

This laconic Jewish wisdom does not take the heights of
encouragement about death that the New Testament does:
Death, the last enemy to our spiritual renewal and revitaliza-
tion, is to be destroyed (I Cor. 15:26). God in Christ has
given us the victory over death in his resurrection. Thanks be
to God for this unspeakable gift! Through our having been
crucified daily with Christ and raised to walk in newness of
life, we have the resurrection as a daily reminder, metaphor,
pattern of living, and manna-like gift to restore us through
rest. Rest itself is the daily foretaste of the resurrection.

Even death itself, then, in the face of the resurrection, is
not a *final* rest. Rest is in the harmony of an eternal rhythm of
rest and creativity.

Jesus and the Gift of Rest

The force that kept me working so compulsively that my
bride asked if I never finished work was and—to a lesser

degree—is the compulsive need to *earn* my way into the approval of God and my neighbor. Though her question was ever so gently put, it was obvious to me that Pauline did *not* expect this of me in order for her to love me. On the contrary, she wanted rest for me. This has always been a parable of God's acceptance of and love for me when I rest.

Jesus came teaching and preaching that the Kingdom of Heaven is here. His message came to a people who were weighed down by the Law as it was minutely interpreted to regulate every small and large act of each day's living. The lawyers, scribes, and Pharisees enforced these rules and regulations of life. A person was in or out of the grace and approval of God, they were told (and they believed), in terms of the way he or she did or did not keep these rules. Their very religion had become an enslavement similar to their slavery in Egypt. Jesus said to the Pharisees and their lawyers:

> But woe to you Pharisees! for you tithe mint, and rue and every herb, and neglect justice and the love of God; these you ought to have done, without neglecting the others. . . . Woe to you lawyers also! for you load men with burdens hard to bear, and you yourselves do not touch the burdens with one of your fingers. (Luke 11:42, 46)

In his own ministry to people carrying such burdens, Jesus said: "Come to me, all who labor and are heavy laden, and I will give you rest" (Matt. 11:28). They were to rest from the grinding load of the official religion of their land and lives. They were to be free of its weight. As Paul said, the letter of the Law kills, but the Spirit gives life. Jesus invited people to follow his way of grace and love, to take his yoke upon them and to learn from him, for he was gentle and lowly in heart,

and they would find rest for their lives. For his yoke was easy
and his burden light (Matt. 11:29–30).

He demonstrated this in his leadership of his disciples.
They traveled through Samaria. In the heat of the day, they
came to a well. While the disciples went for food, Jesus,
"wearied as he was with his journey, sat down beside the
well" at high noon (John 4:6). The Son of God got tired!
When he did, he sat down to rest! In turn he taught his
disciples to do likewise. After they returned from a journey
and a work on which he had sent them, they "told him all that
they had done and taught. And he said to them, 'Come away
by yourselves to a lonely place, and rest a while.' For many
were coming and going, and they had no leisure even to eat"
(Mark 6:31).

You know people today for whom the Christian religion
has been legislated into a massive burden of rules, regulations, and laws. You yourself may be such a person. I have
occasion to see many people whose religion has become a
fear-laden burden. Think of those who, in spite of having
lived scrupulous, exemplary lives, do not believe or feel that
they are "saved." If such persons are Protestant, they are
likely to attend revival after revival and make confession of
faith after confession of faith. If they are Catholic, they may
go from church to church all in the same day and make
confession. These persons carry their religion as an exhausting burden.

Then, again, think of those people who outwardly seem
just the opposite of the overly conscientious people I have
just described. Inwardly, however, they see their religious
memories the same way—as a grievous burden. These persons have compulsively cast aside the external restraints of
their religion and have become compulsive in their sexual
behavior, in their greed for money, in their use of drugs and

alcohol, and in their flaunting and ridiculing of all religion. In a curiously reverse way, they are exchanging one burden for another.

Or think of those who have been through a divorce, although they have been taught by their religion that to be divorced and remarried is to live life in adultery forever. To such persons religion has become a curse rather than a blessing, a burden rather than a renewal and rest. They live their lives with the tacit assumption that they have committed an unpardonable sin.

To all these persons and many more like them the words of Jesus are good news. "Come to me, all who labor and are heavy laden, and I will give you rest" (Matt. 11:28). He gives rest from the unyielding grip of our compulsions. He gives rest from the fear that clutches us. "For God hath not given us the spirit of fear; but of power, and of love, and of a sound mind" (II Tim. 1:7, KJV). The perfect love of God in Christ casts out fear.

My point is that the religious lawyers of the churches of all varieties today have taken the gospel of Christ and made of it a burden of law devoid of grace and wisdom, empty of compassion. Through brainwashing procedures they have bound heavy burdens upon timid people and do not raise a finger to help anyone bear them.

You need not be intimidated any longer by these religious lawyers. Faith in Christ's invitation to rest in his way of grace, wisdom, compassion, and freeing love is the gift he extends to you.

Therefore, both in creation and by command of God in Christ, you are given the gift of rest and commanded to partake of rest as our common grace. We rest in God's approval and in Christ's instruction. Thanks be to God for the renewing gift of rest!

Questions for Thought and Discussion

1. Go to the nearest library and read the article "Fatigue" in Vol. 7 of *The New Encyclopaedia Britannica,* 15th edition, pp. 188–193. Use it as a basis for discussing the way your body functions and fails to do so when you are fatigued.

2. Make a "time study" of one full week. Simply record what you actually *do* each day. Encourage either your family members or a small study group to make their own time studies. Where can you save time for rest?

3. Actually practice the method of Christian meditation in Chapter 4 yourself. Make notes on how you would change it to fit you. Share your reactions with your group—it can be an informal social group in your home. What are their and your practices of "breathing in and breathing out"?

4. What are your personal solutions to unwanted wakefulness? What can you on the basis of Chapter 5 do to add to these solutions?

5. What is the relationship of greed to restlessness, and what disciplines of simplification can you and your group, or your friends, think of that I have not suggested?

6. Can you write down in fewer than fifty words what your basic purpose in life is and what gives you the greatest sense of peace? Try it!

7. Read Heb. 4:1–5 and use this as a way of defining more clearly for yourself what the "prayer of rest" (Chapter 8) can mean to you and your group.

Bibliography

68268

Biblical Resources

Selected Scripture passages bearing on the themes of this book are as follows:

New Testament: Matt. 11:28–29; Mark 6:31; Luke 9:58; 12:19; 23:56; John 4:6; Heb. 4:1–11; Rev. 14:13.

Old Testament: Gen. 1:31 to 2:2; 2:7; Ex. 23:12; 31:15–17; 33:14ff.; Deut. 32:10–11; Ruth 1:9; 3:18; I Chron. 22:9; Job 3:9–19; 20:27; Ps. 51:6; Prov. 14:33; Jer. 6:16; 47:6; Ecclus. 22:11; 30:17.

Books and Journals

Augustine, St. *The Confessions of St. Augustine.* Tr. by John K. Ryan. Doubleday & Co., Image Books, 1960.

Bartley, S. H. "Fatigue," *The New Encyclopaedia Britannica,* Vol. 7. 15th ed. Encyclopaedia Britannica, 1977. Pp. 188–193.

Benson, Herbert. *The Relaxation Response.* William Morrow & Co., 1975.

Buttrick, George Arthur, ed. *The Interpreter's Dictionary of the Bible,* Vol. 4. Abingdon Press, 1962.

Carrington, Patricia. *Freedom in Meditation.* Doubleday & Co., Anchor Press Book, 1978.

Foulkes, David. *The Psychology of Sleep.* Charles Scribner's Sons, 1966.

Hartmann, Ernest, M.D., et al. "Sleep Need: How Much Sleep and What Kind?" *The American Journal of Psychiatry,* Vol. 127, No. 8 (Feb. 1971), pp. 1001–1008.

Jacobson, Edmund. *Anxiety and Tension Control.* J. B. Lippincott Co., 1964.

Kierkegaard, Søren. *Either/Or,* Vol. 2. Tr. by Walter Lowrie. Princeton University Press, 1944.

Merskey, Harold, and Spear, F. G. *Pain: Psychological and Psychiatric Aspects.* London: Bailliere, Tindall & Cassell, 1967.

Noordenbos, W. *Pain: Problems Pertaining to the Transmission of Nerve Impulses Which Give Rise to Pain.* Elsevier Publishing Co., 1959.

Nouwen, Henri J. M. *The Way of the Heart.* Seabury Press, 1981.

Oden, Thomas C., ed. *Parables of Kierkegaard.* Princeton University Press, 1978.

Péguy, Charles. *God Speaks.* Pantheon Books, 1962.

Phillips, E. Lee. *Prayers for Worship.* Word Books, 1979.

Schuyler, Dean. *The Depressive Spectrum.* Jason Aronson, 1974.

Sorensen, Theodore. *Decision-Making in the White House.* Columbia University Press, 1963.

Steere, Douglas. *Work and Contemplation.* Harper & Brothers, 1957.

Stroebel, Charles F., M.D. "Chronopsychophysiology." In *Comprehensive Textbook of Psychiatry/II,* Vol. 1. 2d ed. Ed. by Alfred M. Freedman, M.D., Harold I. Kaplan, M.D., and Benjamin J. Sadock, M.D. Williams & Wilkins Co., 1975. Pp. 166–178.

Tart, Charles, ed. *Altered States of Consciousness.* John Wiley & Sons, 1969.

Tournier, Paul. *A Place for You.* Tr. by Edwin Hudson. Harper & Row, 1968.

U.S. Department of Health, Education, and Welfare. *Work in America: Report of a Special Task Force to the Secretary of Health, Education, and Welfare.* MIT Press, 1973.

Notes